The
Northern
Italian
Cookbook

The Northern Italian Cookbook

by TERESA GILARDI CANDLER

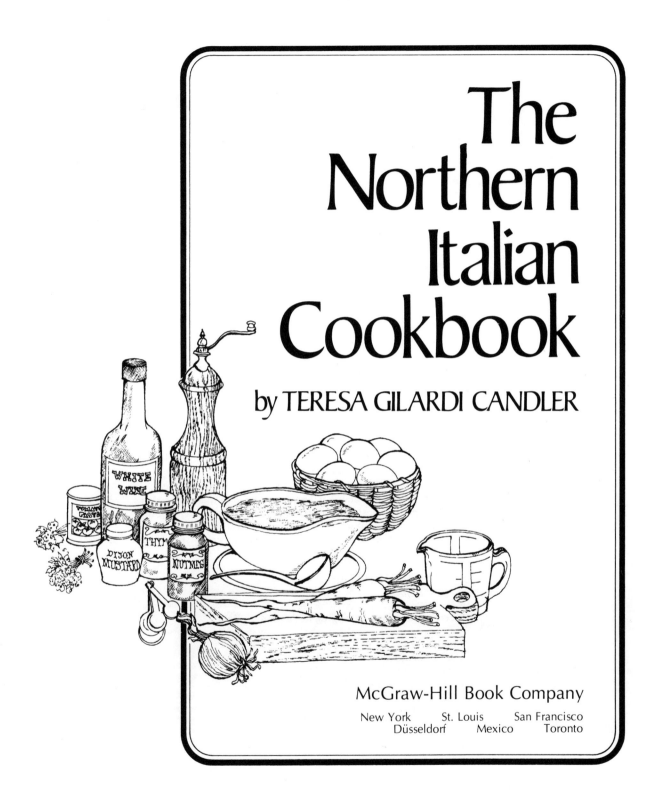

McGraw-Hill Book Company

New York   St. Louis   San Francisco
Düsseldorf   Mexico   Toronto

Book design by Stanley Drate.

Illustrations by Marika.

1 2 3 4 5 6 7 8 9 MUBP 7 8 3 2 1 0 9 8 7

Library of Congress Cataloging in Publication Data

Candler, Teresa Gilardi.
The Northern Italian cookbook.
Includes indexes.
1. Cookery, Italian.   I. Title.
TX723.C2816   641.5′945′1   76-30450
ISBN 0-07-009721-6

To the memory of my parents; to all of the people I love; and to all of those people who love me

Acknowledgments

With the publication of this book I must express my thanks to the many people who have taught me the love for food and cooking—my family, and all the marvelous chefs of Belvedere, my family's restaurant in Torino (Turin), Italy. Also, I am most grateful to all of my friends in Canada, Minnesota, Connecticut, in Rochester, New York, and in New Jersey, where I now enjoy living. With these people, over the years, I have shared the most pleasant and memorable meals; indirectly, they have been responsible for this book's coming into being.

A thanks goes to my son, Peter, for making the long hours at the typewriter more pleasant while he played background music on his piano.

I am particularly grateful to Mr. Craig Claiborne, Mr. Raymond A. Sokolov, and Mrs. Grace Smith for their advice and their support; without their encouragement this book would not have come to be.

Many thanks to Marie Hamm for her assistance in the preparation of my manuscript, and, finally, to my husband, Gerry, whose love and patience helped me through the many hours of toil trying to get the English grammar correct.

To all of you, thanks.

Teresa Gilardi Candler
September, 1976

Contents

Introduction

Another Italian cookbook? Yes, but certainly not a rehash of spaghetti, pizza, tomato sauce, and mozzarella cheese, all abounding with oregano. These Americanized versions do profound injustice to the essential and delicious variety characteristic of the Italian daily table that I know and remember.

To appreciate the diverse nature of Italian cooking we must remember that the people of Italy are descendants of many ancient tribes.

Three thousand years ago, the Etruscans from the eastern shore of the Mediterranean settled in north central Italy and established a flourishing civilization: The founders of Rome, originally from Asia Minor, were refugees of the Trojan War. Eventually they combined with original Italic tribes, and established the Roman Empire and its historic civilization.

The Greeks established prosperous colonies in Sicily and along the coast of Southern Italy. Tribes from the north, east, and west crossed the Alps and became permanent residents of Northern Italy. Later, Normans, Spaniards, and French also settled in the Italian peninsula. Each group contributed ethnic cooking characteristics and practices which were absorbed into the cooking of Italy.

For most of its recent history, Italy has been divided into independent, often rival, and stoically provincial city states, each with regional pride of an intensity that would make Boston, even Texas seem cosmopolitan. Today there are innumerable Italian dialects, distinct life styles, and different eating habits. Remember, too, that Italy has been one country only since 1861— about half as long as the United States.

The recipes presented in this book are from one of the northern regions of Italy, Piemonte e la Valle d'Aosta, an autonomous region of Piemonte. The dishes are indigenous to the region and it is absurd to one of my background to suggest that Piemontese cooking originated in France, as has frequently been charged.

Actually, the opposite is true. Refined French cooking came from Italy in the middle of the 16th century when Caterina de Medici, towing a small battalion of cooks from her native Tuscany, journeyed to France to marry King Henry II.

But this is not a history book, and I'm not a professional writer, nor an historian, and English is not my native language. The purpose of this book is to introduce to the American people the best of present day Northern Italian cooking, and I am grateful to all foreign influences which have made it so exciting.

Thanks to the merchants from Florence, Venice, and Genoa, who after they visited the Orient, introduced exotic spices to Italy and the Western World. Thanks to centuries of housewives, chefs, and others who improved Italian cuisine to its present state of wonderful pleasure.

Many of the recipes in this book represent my family's heritage. They have been patiently collected in the course of three or more generations by my grandmother, my mother and me. Others have been given to me by chefs working in my family's restaurant, the Belvedere, in Torino. There are sophisticated restaurant favorites and family-style dishes. The recipes have been chosen for their simplicity, ingredient availability and compatability with American taste.

All the dishes have been enjoyed by friends who I have had the pleasure of entertaining during my twenty years of residence in the United States. I sincerely hope you will enjoy them too.

II

Piemonte e la Valle d'Aosta

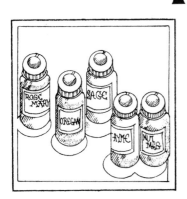

I am proud to introduce to you the dishes of Piemonte. I know Piemonte. I was born there and lived there for many years; my family still lives there. Piemonte is a land-locked region, surrounded by the Alps, with the highest peaks in Europe. It is rich with rivers, lakes, and beautiful hills which are the source of the finest wines of Italy. The capital city is Torino.

In the beautiful Valle d'Aosta, among many specialties, we have *Fontina*, a mild, quick-melting cheese. As you will see, reading through the recipes, it is used in many ways. One of the best of these dishes is *La Fondua*, fondue. When served with the white truffles of Alba, another treasure of the Piemonte soil, it is certainly the best fondue in the world. The Alpine streams offer excellent trout. Perch is abundant in the pre-Alpine lakes. In the rice-growing area there is a good supply of tench, eel, and frogs.

Unbelievably fragrant wild mushrooms are found concealed in dried leaves, bushes and trees of the mountain woods.

The rich pasturelands of Piemonte offer a variety of tasty meats, which are served boiled, roasted, braised, or stewed in a variety of local versions. The *Sanato*, Piemontese milk-fed calf, is the best of Italy. From the same area, fine cheeses are plentiful, *Robiole d'Alba* and *Roccaverano, la Toma d'Aosta*, and *Tomini di Chivasso*, to name a few. The fertile agricultural lands of the Po River Valley produce more than half of Italy's rice, so do not be surprised to find many recipes making use of it, from delicious salads, to soups, and fantastic *Risotto*, an excellent first course dish. It is from this region that, in 1787, Thomas Jefferson allegedly smuggled rice out of Italy to the United States.

Fruits and vegetables are also plentiful in Piemonte. The cherries of Pecetto and Ceresolo, peaches from Casale and the grapes from many vineyards on the hills surrounding Torino add to the good living. The strawberries of S. Mauro provide a special treat each spring. *Martin Sech* is the Piemontese name for a small russet pear from la Valle d'Aosta, delicious when cooked with wine. *Cardi,* a vegetable related to the artichoke, looks like gigantic celery. Its slightly bitter flavor adds interest to Bagna Caôda dipping. You will find them in the Italian vegetable markets in the fall. The regions around the towns of Santena, Poirino and Cambiano produce *Asparagi,* asparagus, of outstanding quality.

Popular *antipasti,* Italian appetizers, are large platters of various cold cuts, and other meats; and rice molds or salads, and mushroom salads; filled and layered *Crespelle;* pickled fish and meats; *Tartine,* small pastry tarts, filled with delicious potpourri; *Crostini,* fried bread, topped with delicate morsels; beautiful and artfully-done aspic dishes. The first course could be *Agnolotti,* filled *ravioli, Tagliatelle,* wide egg noodles, or a variety of *Gnocchi, dumplings,* or *Risotto,* all served with tempting sauces.

An every day family dinner might start with *Minestrone di Verdura,* or a light soup made with a homemade beef or chicken broth.

Bagna Caôda is a sauce served in a casserole over heat, into which every kind of raw or roasted vegetable is dipped. It is little known outside of Piemonte, but the Piemontese love it, and enjoy offering it to their friends, especially in the cold days of winter. I am sure that when you taste it, you will never forget it.

The Piemontese enjoy desserts. Every city, town and village boasts something unusual and excellent. Torino is famous for *Caramelle,* a hard candy; for *Gianduiotti,* hazelnut chocolate candy; for *Galup,* a Piemontese name for a sweet cake made with fruits and a special almond-flavored crust; and for *Bignole,* small filled cream puffs which are, for me, one of the best treats in the world.

Amaretti di Saronno, almond macaroons, *Nocciolini di Chivasso,* tiny hazelnut macaroons, *Biscotti di Novara,* a flat ladyfinger cookie, *Finocchini di Re Francore,* anise cookies, are sweet specialties of Piemonte, not to forget the *Turcet*, a horseshoe-shaped light biscuit, that every baker makes with his own little secret.

A dinner in Piemonte is usually served with one or more wines, from simple but pleasant blends, to prized varieties. One of the best red wines of Italy is *Barolo del Piemonte*, described as "the king of wines and the wine for kings." Less known but equally good among the red wines of Piemonte are, *Nebbiolo, Barbera, Freisa, Grignolino, Gattinara,* and *Dolcetto della Langhe. Asti Spumante,* the celebrated sparkling wine, is the best known of the white wines, but not to be forgotten is the *Moscato d'Asti,* sweet and also sparkling. The *Cortese,* a dry white wine, is always served chilled. *Passito di Caluso,* an aged golden sweet wine, almost like a liqueur, is delicious with fruits and desserts. *Vermouth* is another original product of Piemonte, and is used alone as an *appertivo.* Often, after a meal you would be offered a *digestivo;* this could be one of many country-distilled liquors, such as *Grappa del Piemonte,* similar to brandy, or the aromatic *Genepy,* a liqueur made of mountain herbs. Other times, after a good cup of *espresso, Cognac,* or *Acqua del Po.*

Grissini, the thin breadstick, a familiar specialty of Piemonte, originated in Torino in the 16th century to tempt the appetite of a young and ailing prince.

These are a few of the luscious dishes and wines that the people of Piemonte have developed, with the ingredients available to make each meal a beautiful experience.

III
Some Thoughts and Suggestions about Cooking

T he cooking of Piemonte did not start in the kitchens of the royal palaces and castles. It began in the kitchens of the peasants, where, over an open fire or a wood-burning stove, the women cooked with the ingredients available to them. The ovens were very small in those stoves; most of the time they were filled with apples being baked. Breads and cakes, or any large dish in need of baking, was brought to the local baker's oven. That is why, when you read through the recipes, you will find that many are simple but good to taste and nourishing.

Please do not discard a recipe because you are concerned about calories. Apply the wise philosophy of Piemonte. "The quantity of what you eat is your enemy not the quality; so, eat less of any good thing, but do not give it up. It is not necessary."

It pays to be patient. Always read the recipe in full before you begin its preparation. Time, I think, is a most important factor in good cooking, second only to the good quality of the ingredients.

This is why I tell you to read the recipe first. If you do not have the time required for one particular recipe, choose another. It will not be right if you do not give it the time necessary. And never forget that you can spoil the best of ingredients by over-cooking them.

I sincerely hope that you will not be turned off by recipes with the names in dialect. There are three reasons for giving you these names. First, often it is the only name this recipe has and it cannot be translated. Second, in your travels someday through Piemonte and Valle d'Aosta, you will recognize these names on restaurant menus. Third, these names mean so much to me; they remind me of my early years when more of the dialect was spoken than today.

Talking about herbs, *maggiorana*, marjoram, is for *la cucina del Piemonte* what oregano is for southern Italian cooking. They are of the same family, but marjoram is much milder in flavor. *Dragoncello*, tarragon, *rosmarino*, rosemary; *basilico*, basil; *prezzemolo*, Italian parsley with leaves less curly and less strong in flavor than regular parsley; *salvia*, sage, and *alloro*, bay leaves. These are the herbs frequently used in the *cucina del Piemonte*. When using dried herbs for maximum flavor, crumble them with your fingers before adding to the recipe.

I realize that it is very difficult to find fresh herbs in certain areas and off season, and unless you grow them yourself you will have to use, as I do, the dried varieties. Just remember, if you use the fresh herbs, use three times as much of the amount of the dried variety called for in the recipe. Please do not use the powdered varieties; they are useless.

You will see many recipes call for wine. I deliberately did not suggest foreign wines because in using California and New York state wines I always have had good results.

One of the best secrets of a delicious soup or sauce is a good-quality beef or chicken broth; but not many of us always have handy a bowl of homemade broth in the refrigerator; we are lucky, however, that our supermarkets offer a large variety of excellent canned broths that are always ready for use.

You will notice as you read through the recipes that the use of tomato sauce or tomato paste is limited. This is one of the big differences between northern and southern Italian cooking. Piemontese recipes often call for fresh tomatoes in very small quantity. For a good part of the year the fresh tomatoes available to us are not sun-ripened. Using them can spoil a good recipe. My experience is that the use of a good brand of canned plum tomatoes, sun-ripened and canned at the best time, means better flavor and better results.

It would have been easy to suggest that you substitute margarine for butter. I do not, however, because butter adds a superior flavor of its own. If for health reasons you cannot use butter, substitute margarine or oil; the result, however, will not be the same. Before using the substitute, decide whether it is necessary. If a recipe calls for three tablespoons of butter, and that recipe will serve 6 people, is that little bit of butter really going to hurt you?

To substitute Fumêt, Piemontese Meat-Base Sauce, page 67, I have suggested through the book the use of beef or chicken bouillon cubes, but they are only a substitution for convenience sake. If you choose to use the sauce, substitute one tablespoon of sauce for one bouillon cube.

For the sake of convenience, some of my recipes call for frozen vegetables. Use fresh vegetables if you wish. One pound of fresh vegetables can be used in place of one 10-ounce package of frozen vegetables.

With much trial and error I have found that lean bacon, or *pancetta* (the same cut as bacon, but not smoked; you will find *pancetta* in most Italian food stores), can substitute for expensive prosciutto when it is to be cooked; and, instead of a poor-quality grated Parmesan cheese, a good Gruyère cheese gives excellent results.

Speaking of rice, *Arborio* is the name for the Italian rice available here; but as you will see in the recipes, I have suggested long-grain rice, which is a good substitute.

When necessary to use olive oil for its definite flavor, I suggest it in the recipes; otherwise a good vegetable oil is most satisfactory.

I believe that it does not take any more time to twist a pepper-mill than to shake a jar of ready-ground pepper, but what a difference in the results!

Semolino is farina or semolina in the United States. Please do not try to substitute for it a pre-cooked or quick-cooking farina, used for breakfast food; it will not work.

I have tried to make these recipes simple so they will work in your kitchen as they do in mine. Cooking *alla Piemontese,* there are no elaborate secrets; but I do urge you to use fresh ingredients, and enough of your time. *"Cucinare con passione"*— cooking with love—will bring good results, lots of satisfaction, and praise.

Buon appetito!

Teresa Gilardi Candler

1

Appetizers and Hors d' Oeuvres

Antipasti, Crostini

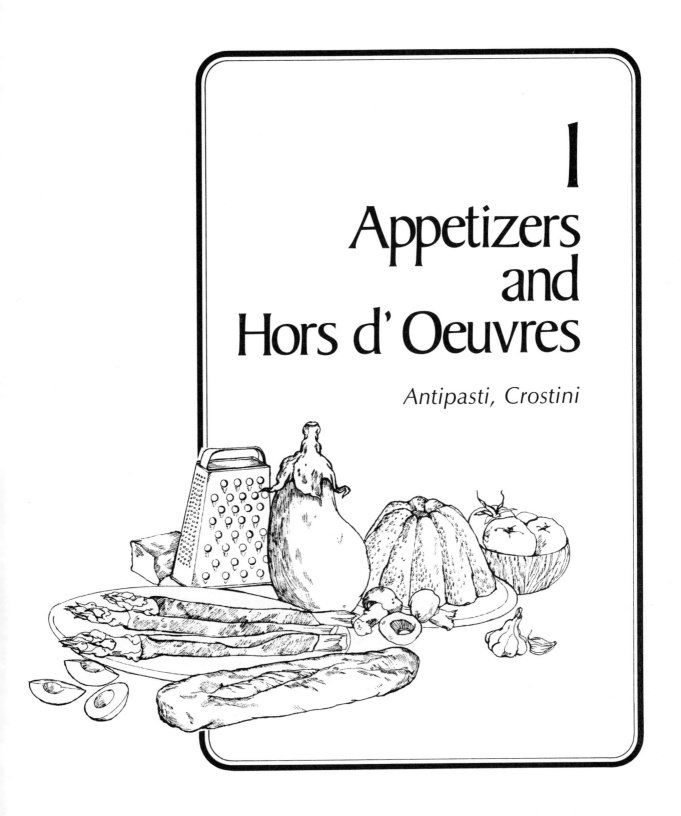

A fat book could be written about *antipasti*. When I recall the artfully prepared dishes at the "Belvedere" my mouth waters. But I am not going to waste words describing them; I will simply give you the recipes. Many of them will make excellent luncheon or salad dishes for your family and friends. Or for your next cocktail party, consider serving a beautiful buffet of hot and cold Italian antipasti and crostini.

PROSCIUTTO AND ASPARAGUS ROLLS
Rotoli di prosciutto e asparagi

12   canned asparagus tips
¼   cup oil
juice one lemon
¼   teaspoon salt
6   slices Italian prosciutto, thinly sliced and cut in half
2   hard-cooked eggs, quartered

Drain asparagus; dry well with paper towels. Arrange in a shallow dish. Mix oil, lemon juice, and salt; pour over asparagus and marinate for 2 hours. Drain well; wrap each asparagus with half slice of prosciutto; arrange in a serving dish; decorate with egg quarters. Serve at room temperature. Serves 4 to 6.

ITALIAN PROSCIUTTO, IRRESISTIBLE
Prosciutto crudo alla golosa

2   tablespoons oil
2   garlic cloves, finely chopped
1   medium onion, peeled and finely chopped
2   red or green sweet fresh peppers, seeded and diced
3   large fresh or canned tomatoes, peeled and chopped
½   teaspoon salt
⅛   teaspoon white pepper
3   tablespoons chopped fresh parsley
12   thin slices Italian prosciutto

In a frying pan, heat oil; add garlic, onion, and peppers; cook until peppers are tender, about 10 to 15 minutes; add tomatoes, salt, pepper, and parsley; simmer uncovered for 45 minutes; cool. Lifting the prosciutto with your fingers, arrange each slice mound-like in a shallow serving dish. Pour sauce over. Serve warm or cold. Serves 6.

BAKED PEPPERS WITH ANCHOVIES
Peperoni al forno
con le acciughe

Preheat oven to 400°F.

 6 fresh red or green peppers
 3 large fresh tomatoes, diced
 3 cloves garlic, thinly sliced
12 anchovy fillets, cut into ½-inch pieces
 3 tablespoons bread crumbs
 3 tablespoons oil
 3 tablespoons butter

Wash peppers, remove seeds and inner core; cut lengthwise into strips 2 inches wide. In a bowl, combine tomatoes, garlic, anchovy fillets, bread crumbs, and oil; mix well. Stuff pepper strips with mixture, arrange on oiled bake-and-serve dish; dot with butter; bake uncovered for 15 minutes. Serves 6.

PICKLED GREEN ONIONS (SCALLIONS)
Cipollini sott' aceto

 4 bunches green onions
½ cup salt
 2 cups white wine vinegar
½ cup oil

Remove top green from onions, leaving about 2 inches of stem above bulb; remove outer skin. In a bowl, cover onions with salt; cover and refrigerate overnight. Next day, wash salt from onions; dry with paper towels. Put them in hot sterilized jars; bring vinegar and oil to a boil and pour hot liquid over onions. Close jars and allow onions to marinate for 2 or 3 days before serving. Serve as an appetizer. Serves 8.

PLUMS WITH BACON ALLA LAURA
Prugne alla Laura

This could be called the Piemontese version of the Hawaiian Rumaki. It is frequently listed on menus through the Aosta Valley.

24 dry plums
2 tablespoons brandy
water to cover plums
12 bacon slices, cut in half

Put plums in a small bowl; pour brandy over and stir; add water just to cover; soak for 20 to 30 minutes. Drain; remove stones carefully; wrap half strip of bacon around each plum, pin with a toothpick. Broil in preheated broiler, turning frequently, until bacon is well done, about 4 to 5 minutes. Remove toothpick, and serve hot with long picks. Serves 6 to 8.

GARLIC BREAD PIEMONTESE
Soma d'ai

This was my favored *merenda* or four o'clock snack, when I was a little girl. It is not served as garlic bread is known in this country; it is a simple appetizing snack. For garlic lovers only.

hard crust rolls or French bread
fresh garlic
oil
salt and pepper

If using French bread, cut the loaf into 5-inch pieces; rub the crust of each piece with garlic, then with oil; sprinkle with salt and pepper and serve. If using hard crust rolls, do not cut; rub the outside of rolls with garlic, oil, salt, and pepper.

HOT ANCHOVY GARLIC DIP
Bagna Caôda

Piemonte is the birthplace of Bagna Caôda, and this is the original Piemontese spelling. This is one of my favorite appetizers. There is an old story that Bagna Caôda was originated as a farmer's lunch during grape harvest time. It could be cooked at home, in an earthenware casserole, then brought to the vineyard where it was kept bubbling hot over an open fire. At noon, the men sat around it, dipping a variety of raw fall vegetables into the sauce.

  1 cup olive oil
  ½ cup butter
  2 2-ounce cans anchovy fillets
 12 cloves garlic, sliced very thin
  1 small truffle (optional)
  ¼ cup heavy cream (optional)
raw vegetable sticks; celery, Savoy cabbage, cauliflower, spinach, peppers, zucchini, and others

Put all ingredients, except vegetables, in an earthenware casserole; simmer very slowly for 1 hour. At the table put casserole over a burner with low flame. Each person dips a selection of raw vegetables into the sauce. Serves 8.

ROASTED PEPPER WITH BAGNA CAÔDA
Peperoni arrostiti con la Bagna Caôda

Canned California roasted peppers are excellent for this recipe.

  1 16-ounce can roasted red peppers
  1 recipe Bagna Caôda, see above
  3 tablespoons red wine vinegar

Rinse peppers with cold water; pat dry with a paper towel. Cut peppers into 1½-inch strips. Mix sauce and vinegar. In shallow dish, arrange peppers and sauce in as many layers as possible; finish with sauce. Cover; let stand at room temperature for 2 or 3 hours before serving. Serves 6 to 8.

**WHIMSICAL
SALAD**
Insalata capricciosa

2 celery roots (knob celery), shredded
½ pound boiled ham, cut into ½-inch strips
½ pound fresh mushrooms, sliced thin
4 small pickled gherkins, chopped
2 tablespoons lemon juice
4 drops Worcestershire
½ teaspoon salt
¼ teaspoon white pepper
½ cup mayonnaise

Combine first four ingredients; sprinkle with lemon juice, Worcestershire, salt, and pepper; blend well. Marinate mixture overnight in refrigerator. Before serving add mayonnaise and blend well. Serves 6 to 8.

**CHICKEN SALAD
"BELVEDERE"**
*Insalata di pollo
"Belvedere"*

6 anchovy fillets, chopped
1 tablespoon prepared mustard
juice of one lemon
¼ cup oil
⅛ teaspoon white pepper
5 large leaves of Boston lettuce, washed and dried
4 chicken breasts, poached, and diced
1 small truffle, sliced very thin (optional)

Combine anchovy fillets, mustard, lemon juice, oil and pepper; mix well and chill for 1 hour. Arrange lettuce in salad bowl; mound chicken in center; spoon dressing over; sprinkle with truffle. Serves 6.

**ANCHOVY
FILLETS IN
GREEN SAUCE**
Acciughe al verde

1 cup finely chopped fresh parsley
3 cloves garlic, finely chopped
2 tablespoons capers, chopped
¼ cup oil, plus oil drained from canned anchovies
4 tablespoons vinegar
½ teaspoon white pepper
4 2-ounce cans anchovy fillets, oil reserved

In small bowl, mix parsley, garlic, capers, oil, vinegar and pepper; blend well with a fork. Layer anchovy fillets in small shallow dish, covering each layer with some of green sauce. Finish with sauce. Cover tightly and refrigerate for 2 or 3 days before using. Anchovies in sauce will keep up to 4 weeks. Serves 6 to 8.

CANAPES
Crostini

Italian Crostini are thin slices of bread cut in various shapes, fried in butter, then topped with a variety of spreads. I have, however, substituted a variety of crackers and Melba toast for Crostini, and have found them thoroughly satisfying.

CHICKEN LIVER CANAPES "BELVEDERE"
Crostini di fegatini di pollo "Belvedere"

3 tablespoons butter
1 pound chicken livers
½ pound fresh mushrooms, thinly sliced
½ cup onions, thinly sliced
1 teaspoon salt
¼ teaspoon black pepper
½ cup dry white wine
1 clove garlic, minced
¼ teaspoon dried rosemary leaves, crumbled
½ cup butter, softened

Melt 3 tablespoons butter in a frying pan; add chicken livers, mushrooms, onions, salt and pepper; sauté for 5 minutes, stirring occasionally. Add wine, garlic, and rosemary. Cover and simmer for 15 minutes. Uncover and continue cooking until almost all liquid has evaporated. Put through a blender for one minute; add softened butter; blend well for one more minute. Transfer to a bowl, cover and refrigerate overnight. Serve on Crostini, crackers or Melba toast. Makes 2 cups.

ANCHOVY CANAPES
Crostini all'acciuga

1 8-ounce package cream cheese
¼ cup anchovy paste
1 tablespoon chopped fresh parsley
1 tablespoon chopped fresh chives

Whip cream cheese in an electric mixer 1 to 2 minutes; add anchovy paste, parsley, chives and mix to a smooth spread. Spread on thin toast or unsalted crackers. Makes 1¼ cups.

CHEESE CANAPES
Crostini al formaggio

1 cup mayonnaise
½ cup Fontina or Gruyère cheese, grated
3 tablespoons onion, finely chopped
3 egg whites, well beaten
48 1½-inch rounds of white bread

In a bowl mix mayonnaise, cheese, onion; add egg whites and blend in gently. Using one teaspoon per bread round, spread mixture very carefully to the edge. Broil 6 inches from heat for 2 to 3 minutes. Can be prepared in advance, covered, and refrigerated for 2 or 3 hours before broiling. Makes 48.

MUSHROOM CANAPES
Crostini ai funghi

1 pound fresh mushrooms
2 tablespoons butter
3 tablespoons dry white wine
1 tablespoon chopped fresh parsley
1 tablespoon chopped fresh chives
½ teaspoon salt
¼ teaspoon black pepper
mayonnaise

Wash mushrooms and cut into small pieces; melt butter in a saucepan; add mushrooms, wine, parsley, chives, salt and pepper; cook uncovered over low heat for 15 minutes. Drain and cool. Serve on canapés or crackers with mayonnaise. Makes 1 cup.

RUSSIAN SALAD
Insalata Russa

This is an easy-to-make antipasto and very effective if decorated with skill. It is a good summer luncheon dish.

3 large potatoes
1 teaspoon salt
1 10-ounce package frozen sliced carrots
1 10-ounce package frozen peas
1 10-ounce package frozen cut string beans
½ cup white vinegar
6 anchovy fillets, cut into ½-inch pieces
6 hard-cooked eggs, diced
½ cup sour gherkins, diced
1 6½-ounce can tuna fish
1 cup mayonnaise, recipe page 69

Put washed, unpeeled potatoes in a large pot; cover with cold water; add salt; cook until tender but firm. Remove from water, peel, cut into ½-inch cubes, and cool. Meanwhile, in a saucepan, combine carrots, peas, string beans and vinegar in water to cover; bring to a boil and cook for 5 minutes; drain well and cool. In a large bowl combine potatoes, vegetables, anchovy fillets, 4 hard-cooked eggs and gherkins, tuna and mayonnaise; mix gently but thoroughly. Arrange in a 10-inch square or round serving dish; smooth it nicely and decorate with some of the vegetable pieces and remaining 2 eggs, quartered. Serves 12.

HAM ROLLS IN ASPIC
Rotoli di prosciutto in gelatina

one-half recipe Russian Salad, see above
12 slices boiled ham
for aspic:
2 envelopes unflavored gelatine
1 10½-ounce can chicken broth, chilled
¾ cup white vinegar
1 cup water
1 teaspoon salt
¼ teaspoon white pepper

Spread 2 tablespoons of Russian salad on each slice of ham and roll up tightly; set aside. In a saucepan add the gelatine to 1 cup of cold broth to soften. Place over low heat and stir until gelatine is dissolved. Remove from heat, stir in remaining broth, vinegar, water, salt and pepper. Return to low heat for 10 minutes. Pour half of gelatine into a shallow serving dish and chill in the refrigerator until firm. Arrange ham rolls on top of firm gelatine; garnish, if desired, with olives, pimiento or green pepper strips. Carefully cover with remaining gelatine; return to refrigerator until firm. Serves 12. Note: If there is leftover Russian salad, it can be served on a lettuce leaf for an appetizer, or used for the recipe for stuffed tomatoes, below.

TOMATOES STUFFED WITH RUSSIAN SALAD
Pomodori ripieni d'insalata Russa

one-half recipe Russian salad, page 10
  6 large firm fresh tomatoes
salt and pepper
12 large green olives

Prepare Russian Salad, reserving 3 tablespoons of mayonnaise. Refrigerate. Wash and dry tomatoes; cut them in half crosswise; scoop out pulp (add it to your next green salad). Sprinkle cavities of tomatoes with salt and pepper; stuff tomato cases with Russian salad; decorate with dots of mayonnaise and slices of olives. Refrigerate for 1 hour before serving. Serves 6.

VEGETABLE APPETIZER PLATTER
Antipasto di verdure ripiene

Handsome and unusual is this platter of stuffed, baked vegetables. It requires work, but it can be served as a clever main course for a buffet party. Combine as many recipes as you like. Each recipe will serve 6.

Stuffed Artichoke Hearts, recipe below.
Carrot Balls, recipe page 159.
Stuffed Baked Tomatoes, recipe page 169.
Stuffed Baked Onions, recipe page 165.
Grandmother's Stuffed Zucchini, recipe page 171.
Sautéed Asparagus, recipe page 158.
Fried Eggplant, recipe page 162.
Breaded Fried Mushrooms, recipe page 164.

CELERY SALAD SIGNOR ANTONIO

Insalata di sedano,
Signor Antonio

3 bunches celery
6 anchovy fillets, cut into ½-inch pieces
4 hard-cooked eggs, diced
3 tablespoons chopped fresh parsley
½ cup sliced sour gherkins
1 tablespoon chopped fresh basil
¼ pound Italian Parmesan or Gruyère cheese, slivered
⅓ cup oil
3 tablespoons red wine vinegar
¼ teaspoon pepper
salt to taste

Discard leaves and wash celery. Cut bunches in half lengthwise and then into ½-inch slices. Place in a salad bowl; add anchovy fillets, eggs, parsley, gherkins, basil, cheese, oil, vinegar, pepper and salt; toss well. Serves 10 to 12.

STUFFED ARTICHOKE HEARTS

Carciofini ripieni

Preheat oven to 500°F.
4 tablespoons unflavored bread crumbs
5 anchovy fillets, chopped
1 clove garlic, chopped
1 tablespoon chopped fresh parsley
1 tablespoon chopped fresh chives
4 tablespoons oil
1 10-ounce package frozen artichoke hearts, defrosted, well drained

In a small bowl combine bread crumbs, anchovy fillets, garlic, parsley, chives, and oil; mix well. Open artichokes enough to spoon in stuffing; arrange in an oiled baking dish and bake for 5 minutes. Transfer gently to a serving dish and serve hot. Serves 4 to 6.

STUFFED MUSH-ROOMS ALLA VALDOSTANA
Funghi ripieni alla Valdostana

Preheat oven to 400°F.

2	pounds fresh white mushrooms
1	small onion, chopped
1	clove garlic, chopped
4	tablespoons butter
4	tablespoons oil
1	tablespoon chopped fresh parsley
½	cup white dry wine
½	teaspoon salt
¼	teaspoon black pepper
½	cup Fontina cheese, grated

Wash and dry mushrooms; remove and chop stems. In a saucepan, sauté mushroom stems, onion and garlic in 2 tablespoons of butter and 2 tablespoons oil for 5 minutes. Add parsley, wine, salt and pepper; cook over low heat 10 minutes longer. Remove from stove; add cheese and stir well. Fill mushroom caps with mixture. Pour remaining oil in a baking dish; arrange mushrooms stuffed side up; dot with remaining butter. Bake uncovered for 15 or 20 minutes. Serves 6 to 8.

MUSHROOM SALAD PAPÁ COSTANTINO
Insalata di funghi, Papá Costantino

My father's favorite mushroom salad is made with fresh, beautiful "ovoli-funghi reali," an egg-shaped mushroom which is found in the hills of Piemonte.

1 pound fresh white mushrooms
1 small truffle (optional)
juice of two lemons
½ cup oil
3 tablespoons chopped fresh parsley
1 clove garlic, chopped
2 hard-cooked eggs, mashed
3 anchovy fillets, chopped, or ½ tablespoon anchovy paste
salt and pepper to taste

Rinse mushrooms and truffle; pat dry with paper towels and cut into thin slices; transfer to a salad bowl; pour lemon juice over and toss lightly. This will prevent them from turning brown. In a small bowl mix oil, parsley, garlic, eggs, and anchovy fillets. Pour over mushrooms and truffle; toss lightly. Add salt and pepper. Serve immediately. Serves 6.

TWO CHEESE PUFFS
Crostini ai due Formaggi

¼ pound Gruyère cheese, grated
¼ pound Swiss cheese, grated
1 egg
2 tablespoons milk
2 teaspoon Kirsch
1 clove garlic, crushed
⅓ cup flour
1 teaspoon baking powder
½ teaspoon salt
¼ teaspoon white pepper
14 slices white bread
oil for deep frying

In small bowl of electric mixer combine cheeses, egg, milk, Kirsch, garlic, flour, baking powder, salt and pepper; mix at medium speed for 5 minutes. Remove crusts from bread slices; cut each slice into four squares. Spread 2 teaspoons of mixture on each square of bread, spreading it carefully to the edges. Heat oil in a frying pan; fry a few squares at a time, cheese side down first. Turn them once, and cook until golden brown on

both sides, about 1 minute each side. Drain on paper towels.
Serve hot. Makes 56.

COLD RICE MOLD

Sformato di riso, freddo

1½ cups uncooked rice
salt
 2 7-ounce cans small shrimps
 1 7-ounce jar roasted red peppers
 2 stalks celery, diced
 1 cup mayonnaise (homemade is best for this recipe) recipe on page 69
 3 hard-cooked eggs, diced
 2 tablespoons chopped fresh parsley
 1 teaspoon chopped capers
 ¼ pound Fontina or Gruyère cheese, diced
 ½ cup pickled mushrooms, diced
 ¼ teaspoon white pepper

Boil rice in 1 quart of water with 1 teaspoon salt, for 10 minutes; drain and rinse twice in cold water; set aside. In a large bowl, combine shrimps, peppers, celery, mayonnaise, eggs, parsley, capers, cheese, mushrooms, pepper, and salt to taste. Add rice and mix well. Turn the mixture into an oiled 9-inch ring mold; cover and refrigerate overnight. Before serving, unmold and fill the center with crisp lettuce leaves. Serves 6 to 8.

PICKLED MUSHROOMS

Funghi sott' aceto

 5 pounds firm white mushrooms
juice of 3 lemons
 6 cups white wine vinegar
2½ cups water
 6 teaspoons salt
12 bay leaves
20 peppercorns
 6 cloves
 6 cloves garlic
 5 1-quart jars, sterilized
olive oil to fill jars

Remove stems from mushrooms and save for other use. Wash mushroom caps briefly in cold water combined with lemon juice. In a large kettle combine vinegar, water, salt, bay leaves, peppercorns, cloves, and garlic; bring to a boil; add the mushrooms and boil for 5 minutes; drain, and remove garlic. Transfer to sterilized jars; fill with oil. Seal and store in cool place. Allow to age for 4 weeks. Refrigerate after jar is opened. Makes 5 quarts.

TUNA FISH FOAM
Schiuma di tonno

1	6½-ounce can tuna fish
4	tablespoons butter, at room temperature
2	hard-cooked egg yolks
2	tablespoons lemon juice
½	teaspoon salt
⅛	teaspoon white pepper

Drain tuna, combine it with butter, egg yolks, lemon juice, salt and pepper; beat in electric blender until fluffy and creamy. Pour mixture into a small oiled bowl; refrigerate for 2 or 3 hours before serving. Carefully turn from bowl onto a serving dish; serve with crackers. Makes 1 cup.

CRESPELLE WITH TRUFFLES
Crespelle ai tartufi

1½	cups flour
1	cup milk
4	tablespoons melted butter
4	eggs
½	teaspoon salt
¼	teaspoon white pepper
1	tablespoon brandy
8	tablespoons butter, at room temperature
10	anchovy fillets, chopped fine
1	truffle (the size is up to you), thinly sliced

In a bowl combine flour, milk, melted butter, eggs, salt, pepper, and brandy; beat to a smooth batter; cover and set aside at room temperature for 1 to 4 hours, or refrigerate overnight. Heat a 6-inch Teflon-coated skillet; measure batter 2 tablespoons at a time for each crespo; pour batter in skillet, tilting the skillet to cover the bottom completely. Cook crespelle 1 minute on each side, or until lightly golden; transfer to a wooden board to cool. Continue until all the batter is used. Makes 15 to 20. The crespelle could be made the day before and refrigerated with pieces of waxed paper between each crêpes.

Preheat oven to 400°F. In a small bowl, combine 4 tablespoons butter, anchovies, truffle; mix well. Spread some of the truffle mixture over each crespo; roll and place each one seam-side down in a bake-and-serve dish; dot with the remaining 4 tablespoons butter and bake for 15 minutes. Serve hot. Serves 4 to 6.

ROYAL ANTIPASTO "BELVEDERE"

Antipasto di crespelle farcite, "Belvedere"

Crespelle is the Italian name for very thin pancakes. Here they are used to make delicious antipasto for an elegant dinner, or a beautiful luncheon dish. They are better made a day ahead. The crespelle are also used in place of cannelloni or manicotti pasta, stuffed with a variety of fillings. Please read the recipe carefully before beginning.

3	eggs
1	cup flour
½	teaspoon salt
¼	teaspoon white pepper
1	cup milk
3	tablespoons brandy
2	tablespoons oil

In a bowl, beat eggs until foamy; sift in flour mixed with salt and pepper and beat until smooth; stir in milk, brandy and oil. Heat a 12-inch Teflon-coated skillet; measure batter ⅓ of a cup at a time into skillet, tilting skillet to cover bottom completely. Cook crespelle for 1 to 2 minutes on each side, until lightly golden; transfer to a wooden board to cool. Continue until all the batter is used. If crespelle are made in advance, layer them with pieces of waxed paper in between and refrigerate. Makes 10 to 12 crespelle.

For filling:
1   recipe Mayonnaise Sauce, page 69
1   6½-ounce can tuna fish
½   pound cooked ham, sliced thin
1   pound chicken or turkey breast, cooked and thinly sliced
1   6½-ounce can liver pâté
½   pound Fontina or Swiss cheese, sliced thin
1   head of escarole lettuce (use only inside white leaves)
½   pound well-done roast beef, sliced thin

Use one of the above fillings for each layer. Place one crespo on a serving platter; spread it with mayonnaise and use the first filling; add another crespo, another filling, and so on until all the crespelle and fillings have been used.

For trimming:
3   hard-cooked eggs, cut into wedges
6   anchovy fillets
6   black olives, cut in half lengthwise
6   sour gherkins cut into matchstick pieces
2   medium ripe tomatoes, cut in wedges
remaining mayonnaise

Cover the tower of crespelle with mayonnaise, and decorate as your artistic talent suggests. Gently cover with plastic wrap and refrigerate at least 2 hours before serving. Cut into wedges. Serves 10 to 12.

RAW BEEF SALAD PIEMONTESE
Insalata di carne, cruda alla Piemontese

2   pounds ground top-quality beef or veal fillet
juice of four lemons
½   cup oil
2   cloves garlic, finely chopped
salt and pepper to taste

Put meat in deep serving plate; cover with lemon juice, add oil, garlic, salt and pepper; mix well and refrigerate for 2 or 3 hours before serving. Stir occasionally to mix. Serve in a mound with lemon wedges. For those who prefer very rare meat, add lemon juice 15 minutes before serving. Serves 4 to 6.

RAW BEEF SALAD LAURA

Insalata di carne cruda alla Laura

2 pounds raw beef or veal fillets, sliced paper thin
juice of two lemons
½ teaspoon salt
¼ teaspoon white pepper
¼ cup olive oil
½ pound bulk Parmesan cheese, slivered

In an oiled, shallow serving dish, arrange a layer of meat; sprinkle with a portion each of lemon juice, salt, pepper, oil and cheese; continue layering and seasoning, ending with a top layer of cheese. Refrigerate 2 or 3 hours before serving. Serves 4 to 6.

RAW BEEF AND MUSHROOM SALAD SIGNOR ANTONIO

Insalata di carne cruda con funghi, Signor Antonio

This is the beef salad version of Signor Antonio, one of the chefs of the "Belvedere." He worked with my father for many years, and I am certainly indebted to him, not only for his recipes, but for his patience while teaching me the art of cooking.

1 pound firm, white mushrooms (use only the caps save the stems for other use)
juice of two lemons
2 pounds sliced raw beef or veal fillet, sliced paper thin
½ teaspoon salt
¼ teaspoon white pepper
½ pound bulk Parmesan cheese, slivered
¼ cup olive oil

Wash and dry mushroom caps; slice ⅛ inch thick; arrange in a shallow serving dish; sprinkle with 2 tablespoons lemon juice; arrange meat over mushrooms; sprinkle with remaining lemon juice, salt and pepper. Cover with cheese and pour oil over. Cover dish with plastic film and set aside for 30 minutes before serving. Do not refrigerate. Serves 4 to 6.

2
Soups

Minestre

C an there be a more delightful aroma in a kitchen than that of an old-fashioned soup simmering on the back burner of the stove? Even today, in my modern American kitchen, rarely a day goes by that my family is not greeted by some mouth-watering soup fragrance. It may be a vegetable soup today, a simple chicken broth with young peas tomorrow, or an extra thick vegetable soup with rice.

Steaming hot soup comforts the Piemonte spirit when the weather is cold. The summertime soups are served either at room temperature or chilled.

PIEMONTESE VEGETABLE SOUP

Minestrone di verdure alla Piemontese

There are three variations of the Minestrone di verdure alla Piemontese; one, the classic vegetable soup; second, with the addition of small macaroni; the third with rice. The second and third are good cold soups for a summer dinner. An Italian cold soup is never served deeply chilled as you would serve Gazpacho or Vichyssoise, but at room temperature.

1	pound dried Great Northern white beans
½	cup oil
5	slices bacon, chopped
2	cloves garlic, chopped
1	large onion, chopped
4	carrots, diced
6	celery stalks, diced
1	8-ounce can plum tomatoes
1	tablespoon chopped fresh basil
1	tablespoon chopped fresh parsley
2	cups peeled and diced potatoes
4	medium zucchini, diced
½	pound fresh green beans, cut into ½-inch pieces
1	small Savoy cabbage, shredded
2	quarts home-made or canned beef broth
½	cup grated Parmesan cheese
½	teaspoon black pepper
	salt to taste

Cover washed beans with water; soak overnight. In a small skillet, cook oil, bacon, garlic, and onion over medium heat for 10 minutes, stirring occasionally. Drain beans and put into a large kettle; add bacon-onion mixture, carrots, celery, tomatoes and juice, basil, parsley, potatoes, zucchini, green beans, cabbage and broth; cover and simmer for 3 to 4 hours. Before serving, stir in the cheese, pepper, and salt. Serves 10 to 12.

VEGETABLE SOUP, HOT OR COLD
Minestrone di verdure, caldo o freddo

Prepare vegetable soup as for "Piemontese Vegetable Soup," page 23. Before serving, add either rice or small macaroni of your choice. To serve it cold, make the soup in the morning; leave it on top of the cold stove, and serve at room temperature at dinner time.

For Rice: In a small saucepan bring to a boil 3 cups of water with ½ teaspoon salt; add 1 cup of uncooked long-grain rice and boil for 8 minutes. Drain and add to the soup before serving.

For Small Macaroni: Cook 1 cup of small macaroni in 4 cups of water with 1 tablespoon salt, for 10 minutes; drain and add to the soup before serving.

ROYAL CHICKEN SOUP
Minestrina reale

Some of the princes and kings of the Savoy dynasty were famous "bon vivants," in the habit of enjoying what the region had to offer, perhaps a beautiful woman, a great wine, or a great dish. It was quite natural to honor a dish which had pleased royalty with the name "reale."

1	cup chicken breast meat, cooked and finely chopped
2	egg yolks
½	teaspoon salt
⅛	teaspoon nutmeg
4	cups homemade or canned chicken broth
4	tablespoons grated Parmesan cheese

In a small bowl combine chopped chicken breast, egg yolks, salt, and nutmeg; mix well. Bring broth to a boil; remove from stove; add chicken mixture and cheese; stir vigorously for 2 or 3 minutes. Serve immediately. Serves 4 to 6.

LENTIL SOUP
Minestra di lenticchie

2	pounds pork neck bones
7	cups water
1½	cups dried lentils
1	stalk celery, diced
5	carrots, diced
1	large onion, chopped
2	teaspoons salt
½	teaspoon black pepper
4	bay leaves

In a large kettle combine all ingredients; cover, bring to a boil; lower heat and simmer for 2 hours. Remove meat from bones and return it to the soup. Serve hot. Serves 6 to 8.

POTATO, CHIVES, AND LEEK SOUP
Minestra di patate porri e erba cipollina

This soup is excellent served hot or cold. To chill, cool in refrigerator for one hour before serving.

6	cups canned chicken broth
4	large leeks, sliced
1½	pounds potatoes, peeled and diced
1	teaspoon salt
¼	teaspoon white pepper
¼	cup chopped fresh or frozen chives

In a large kettle, combine broth, leeks, potatoes and seasonings; cover and bring to a boil. Lower heat and simmer for 1½ hours. Transfer cooked vegetables to a blender and purée. Return to kettle; add chives and simmer for 5 minutes longer. Serves 6 to 8.

BAKED BREAD SOUP

Minestra mitunnà

Preheat oven to 400°F.

4 tablespoons butter
8 slices Italian bread or one-day-old white bread
1 cup grated Parmesan cheese
8 eggs
3 cups hot beef broth (you can use canned broth for this recipe)
Salt and pepper to taste

Melt butter in a large skillet; fry slices of bread on both sides, until golden; transfer to a large bake-and-serve dish, or individual ramekins; sprinkle with cheese. Break eggs over bread and very carefully pour hot broth over it. Add salt and pepper. Serve immediately. Serves 4.

BEEF TRIPE SOUP

Minestra di trippa alla Piemontese

½ cup butter
¼ cup ham fat, chopped
1 large onion, chopped
2 leeks, white part only, sliced
3 pounds honeycomb beef tripe, cleaned and cooked (it usually comes cooked)
2 stalks celery, diced
3 carrots, diced
3 medium potatoes, peeled and diced
1 cup Great Northern dried beans, boiled separately for 1 hour
6 canned plum tomatoes, chopped
1 small Savoy cabbage, shredded
1 clove garlic, minced
2 teaspoons salt
1 teaspoon black pepper
4 quarts water
1 cup grated Parmesan cheese

Place butter and ham fat in a large kettle; add onion and leeks; brown lightly. Add all ingredients except cheese. Cover kettle; bring to a boil; lower heat and simmer for 2 hours. Remove from heat; add cheese; stir and serve. Serves 8 to 10.

CHESTNUT SOUP
Minestra di castagne

(Children may like this soup more with the addition of a little sugar in their own bowl.)

½   pound peeled dried chestnuts
1   small onion, whole
1   stalk celery, cut into large pieces
1   small carrot, whole
4   cups milk
2   cups water
1   teaspoon salt
⅛   teaspoon white pepper
⅛   teaspoon nutmeg
½   cup uncooked rice

In a bowl, cover chestnuts with lukewarm water; soak overnight. The following day, drain chestnuts; place in a large saucepan; add onion, celery, carrot, milk, water, salt, pepper, and nutmeg. Bring to a boil; lower heat, cover and simmer for 1 hour. Remove and discard onion, celery, and carrot. Add the rice; cook for 10 minutes longer and serve. Serves 4 to 6.

BARLEY AND BEEF SOUP
Minestra d'orzo con manzo

2   pounds beef short ribs
7   cups water
1   large onion, sliced
1   8-ounce can plum tomatoes with juice
6   carrots, diced
4   celery stalks, sliced
2   teaspoons salt
½   teaspoon black pepper
1   cup dried barley

Put beef in a large kettle; add water, onion, tomatoes, carrots, celery, salt, pepper, and barley. Cover, bring to a boil; lower heat and simmer for 2½ to 3 hours. Remove meat from bones;

cut half of it into small pieces and add to the soup. Use remaining beef for beef salad. Simmer 10 minutes longer and serve hot. Serves 6 to 8.

SPLIT PEA SOUP
Minestra di piselli secchi

3 tablespoons butter
3 tablespoons oil
3 thin slices boiled ham, diced
4 scallions with green tops, thinly sliced
6 cups canned or homemade chicken broth
6 cups water
2 cups dried split green peas
1 teaspoon salt
½ teaspoon white pepper
¼ cup grated Parmesan cheese

In a small skillet, combine butter and oil; add ham and scallions; cook over medium heat until golden. Transfer to a large kettle; add broth, water, peas, salt and pepper. Cover. Bring to a boil; lower heat and simmer for 2 to 3 hours. Before serving stir in the cheese. Serve hot. Serves 6.

TOMATO SOUP ALLA TORINESE
Minestra di pomodoro alla Torinese

1 pound sun-ripened tomatoes, *or* 1 16-ounce can plum tomatoes, chopped
1 clove garlic
4 or 5 leaves fresh basil
1 tablespoon fresh lemon juice
1 tablespoon sugar
1 teaspoon salt
¼ teaspoon white pepper
2 tablespoons butter
2 tablespoons flour
4 cups homemade or canned chicken broth, heated

In a saucepan combine tomatoes with juice, garlic, basil, lemon juice, sugar, salt and pepper; cover and bring to a boil. Lower heat and simmer 30 minutes. Pour into blender container and purée. Melt butter in same saucepan; blend in flour; gradually add chicken broth, stirring constantly; cover and cook over low heat for 10 minutes. Add tomato purée to broth; cook over low heat 10 minutes longer. Serve hot or thoroughly chilled. Serves 6.

LITTLE SOUP WITH CHICKEN LIVERS AND PEAS
Minestrina al brodo con fegatini di pollo e piselli

Minestrina is the name used for light soups made with broth and any small macaroni.

1   pound fresh peas, or 1 10-ounce package frozen peas, thawed
2   tablespoons butter
10   chicken livers, chopped
4   cups homemade or canned chicken broth
½   cup small macaroni (little stars, seeds, or rings)
salt and pepper to taste
Parmesan cheese

If using fresh peas remove from shells. Melt butter in a saucepan; add chicken livers and sauté for 5 minutes; add peas and cook over low heat for 5 minutes. Pour in broth; bring to a boil; add macaroni and cook for 10 minutes. Add salt and pepper if needed. Serve hot with cheese in a separate bowl. Serves 4 to 6.

BROCCOLI SOUP WITH RICE
Minestra di broccoli e riso

1   bunch fresh broccoli, 1½ pounds, chopped
1   cup chopped onions
3   leeks, white only, chopped
2   pounds potatoes, peeled and diced
5   cups homemade or canned beef broth
4   tablespoons butter
⅓   cup long-grain rice
¼   cup grated Parmesan cheese
salt and pepper to taste

In a large kettle, place broccoli, onions, leeks, potatoes, and broth; bring to a boil. Cover; lower heat and simmer for 1 hour. Transfer all vegetables to a blender and purée. Return to kettle; add butter and rice; stir, and cook slowly, covered, for 10 to 15 minutes; rice should be tender but firm. Add cheese, salt, and pepper. Serve hot. Serves 6 to 8.

PORK AND BEAN SOUP
Tofeja

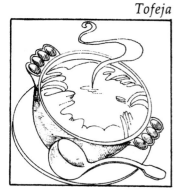

This soup is a dish of Canavese, a region of Piemonte at the foot of d'Aosta Valley. It takes its name from a clay-pot in which it is cooked. It is best used as a heavy soup for a one-dish dinner accompanied by a tossed salad.

Preheat oven to 250°F.
1 pound dried Great Northern beans
2 cloves garlic
1 teaspoon dried rosemary leaves
3 teaspoons salt
1 teaspoon black pepper
½ teaspoon grated nutmeg
1 pound fresh pork rind
2 pigs feet, cut into 2-inch pieces
1 medium onion
4 bay leaves
4 dried sage leaves, crumbled
2 celery stalks, sliced
1 carrot, diced

Place the beans in a bowl; cover with warm water and soak overnight. The following morning, mince together 1 clove garlic and rosemary; mix in ½ teaspoon salt, pepper, and nutmeg. Wash pork rind; pat dry and cut into 3 × 5-inch pieces; sprinkle a portion of garlic-rosemary seasoning on each; roll up and tie with string. Set aside. Drain beans; transfer to a clay bean-pot. Add pork rind rolls, pigs feet, onion, bay and sage leaves, remaining clove garlic, chopped, and salt, celery, and carrot. Cover with boiling water; cover pot tightly and bake for 4 to 5 hours, until beans are tender. Serves 6 to 8.

ASTI'S BEAN SOUP
Minestra di fagioli all'Astigiana

2   cups dried Great Northern beans
3   quarts water
1   small onion
2   carrots, diced
3   stalks celery, diced
1   clove garlic, whole
2   cloves
4   sprigs fresh parsley
2   teaspoons salt
½   teaspoon white pepper
6   tablespoons butter
3   tablespoons oil
3   slices white bread, each cut into four triangles
½   cup grated Parmesan cheese

Wash beans; put them into a bowl; cover with water and soak overnight. The following morning drain the beans; put in a large kettle; add water, onion, carrots, celery, garlic, cloves, parsley, salt, pepper, 3 tablespoons butter, and oil. Cover; bring to a boil; lower heat and simmer 2 to 3 hours. Drain liquid into a bowl, and set aside. Force beans and vegetables through a food strainer, or purée in blender; combine liquid and purée in kettle; simmer for a few minutes to heat through. Meanwhile fry bread triangles in remaining butter. Put two in each soup bowl; pour soup over and serve with the cheese in a separate bowl. Serves 6 to 8.

RICE AND MILK SOUP
Minestra di riso al latte

5   cups milk
¾   cup long-grain rice
1   teaspoon salt
3   tablespoons butter

In a kettle, heat 4 cups of milk just to boiling; reduce heat at once. Add rice and salt; stir and cook over low heat until almost all of the milk is absorbed, about 15 to 20 minutes. Warm remaining 1 cup milk with butter and add to cooked rice; stir and serve hot. Serves 4 to 6.

RICE AND POTATO SOUP ALLA CANAVESE
Minestra di riso e patate alla Canavese

3 slices bacon, chopped
1 clove garlic, chopped
4 medium potatoes, peeled and diced
4 canned plum tomatoes
1 teaspoon salt
½ teaspoon white pepper
3 bay leaves
2 quarts water
1 cup long-grain rice
3 tablespoons grated Parmesan cheese

In a small frying pan, brown bacon with garlic; transfer to a kettle; add potatoes, tomatoes, salt, pepper, bay leaves, and water; heat to boiling; lower heat, cover and simmer for 30 minutes. Add rice; heat to boiling, lower the heat, cover and simmer for 20 minutes longer. Discard bay leaves. Remove from heat; stir in cheese and serve hot. Serves 6.

NOVARA RICE SOUP
Paniscia di Novara

Even if Novara is only a few miles from Vercelli, the dialects are different and so is the rice soup.

1 cup dried large lima beans
3 quarts water
1 teaspoon salt
½ teaspoon black pepper
2 stalks celery, diced
1 carrot, diced
1 small Savoy cabbage, shredded
1 cup canned plum tomatoes, chopped
½ pound fresh pork rind, cut into 1-inch squares
1 medium onion
4 ounces lard
4 tablespoons butter
2 cups long-grain rice
1 cup Barbera (red) or dry white wine

Soak the beans in warm water overnight. The following morning drain and transfer to a large kettle; add water, salt, pepper, celery, carrot, cabbage, tomatoes, and pork rind. Cover kettle; heat to boiling; lower heat and simmer for 3 hours. Meanwhile, chop onion with lard. Melt butter in a large frying pan; add onion and lard; fry until onion is golden; add the rice; cook over medium heat for 2 or 3 minutes stirring constantly. Add wine and cook until wine has evaporated. Stir rice into vegetable mixture in kettle; turn off the heat and let stand covered for 10 minutes. Add salt and pepper to taste. Serve hot. Serves 6 to 8.

VERCELLI RICE SOUP
Panissa di Vercelli

Panissa is a bean and rice soup, a specialty of Vercelli, the rice capital of Italy.

1   cup dried large lima beans
6   cups canned beef broth
1   pound ground lean pork
½   teaspoon black pepper
1   large onion
¼   pound fresh lard
2   tablespoons oil
2   cups long-grain rice
½   cup grated Parmesan cheese
salt to taste

Soak beans in warm water overnight. The following morning, drain beans and transfer to a large kettle; add broth, pork, and pepper; cover and heat to boiling; lower heat and simmer for 2 hours. Meanwhile, chop onion with lard. Heat oil in large frying pan; add lard-onion mixture and cook until onion is golden; add rice and stir; cook over medium heat for 2 or 3 minutes, stirring constantly. Add some of the broth from bean mixture; cook, uncovered, over medium low heat stirring often; as rice absorbs liquid, add more broth. Do not cook longer than 15 to 20 minutes. The panissa should be creamy, not dry. Remove from heat; add cheese; stir and add salt to taste. Serve immediately. Serves 6 to 8.

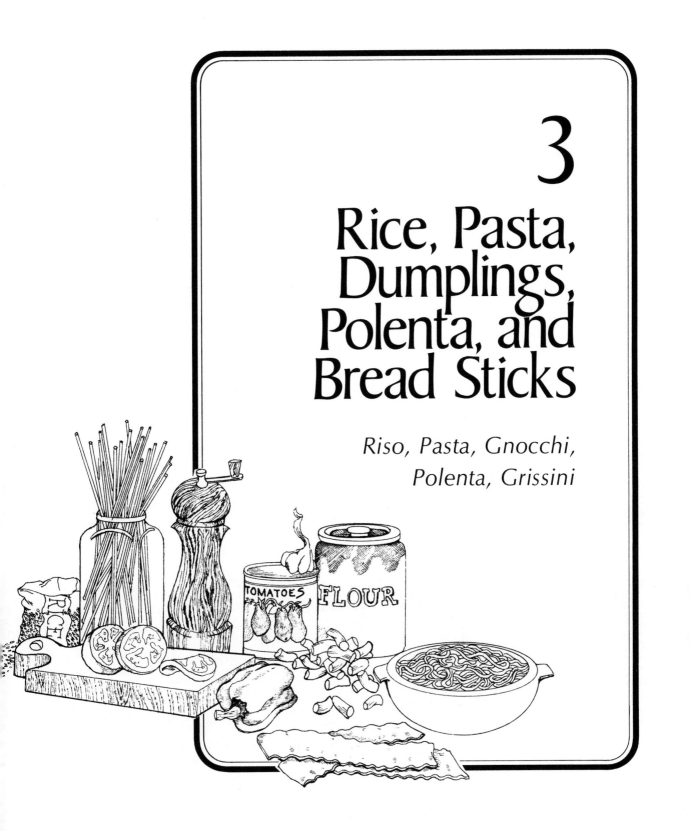

3

Rice, Pasta, Dumplings, Polenta, and Bread Sticks

Riso, Pasta, Gnocchi,
Polenta, Grissini

Occasionally I substitute one of many ways of preparing rice, of which the Piemontese are very fond, or a dish of cream of wheat dumplings, or polenta for the soup course.

Italian rice has a superior long-grain quality. When the grains are cooked to perfection, they should have a creamy consistency on the outside but still be firm on the inside. For best results for the rice recipes in this book, use a good-quality long-grain rice.

Until a few years ago, the pasta consumed in the Piemontese homes was home-made egg noodles, but not so today. Noodle making is a time-consuming project, and now good freshly-made or dried noodles and other pastas are found in local stores.

RICE
Riso

RICE WITH SAGE BUTTER
Riso alla salvia

4	tablespoons butter
1½	teaspoons dried sage leaves, crumbled
2	cups homemade or canned chicken broth
2	cups water
1½	cups long-grain rice
½	cup grated Parmesan cheese

Melt butter in a small saucepan; add sage; cover and cook over very low heat for 15 minutes. Meanwhile, in another saucepan, combine broth and water; heat to boiling; add rice, lower heat and simmer uncovered until rice is tender but firm, about 12 to 14 minutes. Drain if necessary and transfer to a warm serving bowl. Through a strainer, pour hot butter over rice. Top with cheese; stir and serve immediately. Serves 4 to 6.

RICE WITH EGG YOLKS
Riso all'uovo

2 cups homemade or canned chicken broth
2 cups water
1½ cups long-grain rice
4 tablespoons butter, at room temperature
4 egg yolks
½ cup grated Parmesan cheese

In a saucepan, heat broth and water to boiling; add rice; lower heat and simmer uncovered 10 to 14 minutes, until rice is tender but firm; drain, if necessary. Transfer to a heated serving bowl; add butter and stir well. Add one egg yolk at a time stirring constantly; stir in cheese. Serve immediately. Serves 4 to 6.

RICE WITH SPUMANTE
Risotto allo Spumante

One of Italy's great pleasures and prides is a sweet, sparkling white wine, Asti Spumante. It is served with desserts and for special occasions. Here, it is used in an elegant rice dish.

2 tablespoons butter
2 tablespoons oil
1 small onion, chopped
1 celery stalk, chopped
1½ cups long-grain rice
2 cups homemade or canned chicken broth, heated
2 cups dry Asti Spumante
3 tablespoons butter
½ cup grated Parmesan cheese
Salt to taste

Heat butter in a skillet; add oil, onion and celery; cook until soft, about 5 minutes. Add rice, stir until well coated. Add 1 cup broth, stir and cook over low heat. As broth becomes absorbed, add more broth; then, add Spumante a little at a time; continue to cook until rice is tender, about 15 to 20 minutes; rice should be creamy but firm. Before serving, stir in 3 tablespoons of butter, cheese and salt. Serves 6.

RICE WITH PIEMONTESE FONDUE
Risotto con la fonduta Piemontese

2 cups homemade or canned chicken broth
2 cups water
1½ cups long-grain rice
½ recipe for Piemontese cheese fondue, page 150

In a saucepan combine broth and water; heat to boiling; add rice; lower heat, and simmer uncovered for 8 to 14 minutes, until rice is tender but firm. Meanwhile, prepare fondue. Drain rice and transfer to a warm serving bowl; pour fondue over. For special occasions top with a finely sliced small truffle. Serve hot. Serves 4 to 6.

RICE WITH ITALIAN SAUSAGE
Risotto con salciccia

"Salciccia" is a sweet, fresh sausage, about 1 inch in diameter and several feet long.

6 tablespoons butter
2 tablespoons oil
1 medium onion, chopped
1 small carrot, chopped
½ stalk celery, chopped
1 pound sweet Italian sausage, cut into 3-inch pieces
½ cup white dry wine
1½ cups long-grain rice
2 cups homemade or canned beef broth
2 cups water
2 tablespoons tomato paste
½ cup grated Parmesan cheese

Heat 2 tablespoons butter in a large skillet; add oil, onion, carrot, and celery; sauté for 5 minutes; add sausage and brown lightly; add wine and cook for 15 minutes. Pour off sausage fat; add rice; sauté for 2 or 3 minutes, stirring frequently. In saucepan, combine broth, water, and tomato paste; bring to a boil; lower heat so broth barely simmers. Pour one cup of broth into rice mixture; stir and cook gently; continue adding broth before it is all absorbed, ½ cup at a time, until rice is tender—creamy outside but still firm inside. Remove from heat; add remaining 4 tablespoons butter and cheese; stir; transfer to a warm serving dish and serve immediately. Serves 6.

RICE WITH RED OR YELLOW PEPPERS

Risotto con peperoni, Rissi o gialli

4	tablespoons oil
1	small onion, sliced
1	celery stalk, chopped
3	red or yellow peppers, cut into 2-inch pieces
1	8-ounce can plum tomatoes, drained and chopped
4	leaves fresh or ½ teaspoon dried basil
½	teaspoon salt
¼	teaspoon black pepper
1½	cups long-grain rice
2	cups homemade or canned chicken broth
4	tablespoons butter

In a large skillet, heat the oil; add onion, celery, and peppers; cover and cook over medium heat for 30 minutes. Stir in tomatoes, basil, salt, pepper, rice and chicken broth. Cover and cook over low heat for 30 minutes, stirring occasionally. Add a little warm water as needed. When rice is tender-firm, transfer to a warm serving bowl; stir in butter and serve immediately. Serves 6.

RICE WITH A SAUCE OF THREE CHEESES

Risotto ai tre formaggi

½	cup heavy cream
1	3-ounce package cream cheese
3	ounces Gorgonzola cheese (Italian bleu cheese)
½	cup grated Parmesan cheese
⅛	teaspoon nutmeg
2	cups homemade or canned chicken broth
2	cups water
1½	cups long-grain rice

In double boiler, over simmering water, combine cream, cream cheese and Gorgonzola; stir constantly with a wooden spoon, until cheeses are melted. Remove from heat; add Parmesan cheese and nutmeg. Meanwhile, in a saucepan, heat broth and water to boiling; lower heat, add rice and simmer, uncovered, for 12 to 15 minutes, until rice is tender but firm. Drain if necessary and transfer rice to a warm serving bowl; pour cheese sauce over; stir gently and serve immediately. Serves 6.

RICE WITH FRESH TOMATOES
Risotto con pomodori freschi

3	tablespoons butter
1½	cups long-grain rice
1	pound sun-ripened tomatoes, or 1 16-ounce can plum tomatoes, chopped
1½	teaspoons salt
2	teaspoons sugar
¼	teaspoon white pepper

In saucepan, melt butter; add rice and stir until coated. If using fresh tomatoes, add 1½ cups of water; if using canned tomatoes, measure liquid from tomatoes and add water to measure 2 cups. Add liquid, tomatoes, salt, sugar, and pepper to rice. Cover; cook over low heat for 15 to 20 minutes, until the rice is tender-firm. Transfer to a warm serving bowl and serve immediately. Serves 6.

RICE WITH WILD MUSHROOMS
Risotto trifolato con funghi selvatici

The word *trifola* in the Piemontese dialect means "truffle" and the word *trifolato* means "with truffles."

The first people to eat truffles were the Italian farmers who found them in the woods. When truffles became a luxury, even for the wealthy, a combination of wild mushrooms, parsley, garlic, and butter became popular. Even though it bears little relationship to the taste and texture of truffles, this sauce adds delicious interest at moderate cost.

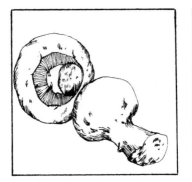

2 ounces wild dried mushrooms
2 cups homemade or canned chicken broth
4 tablespoons butter
1½ cups long-grain rice
4 tablespoons oil
1 clove garlic, finely chopped
½ teaspoon salt
¼ teaspoon black pepper
2 tablespoons finely chopped fresh parsley
½ cup grated Parmesan cheese

Soak mushrooms in 2 cups lukewarm water for one hour; reserve soaking water. Rinse mushrooms and drain; cut them into small pieces, and set aside. Filter mushroom water through a piece of cloth; combine with broth in a saucepan; heat to boiling; lower heat until broth barely simmers. Melt 2 tablespoons butter in a large skillet; add rice and stir until well coated. Add one cup of broth; stir and cook gently; continue adding broth before it is all absorbed and cooking, until rice is tender-firm. Meanwhile, in a skillet heat remaining butter; add oil, and sauté garlic for 2 or 3 minutes; add mushrooms, salt, and pepper; stir and cook at medium heat for 8 to 10 minutes. Add parsley and remove from heat. Transfer cooked rice to a warm serving bowl; spoon mushrooms over; top with cheese and serve immediately. Serves 6.

RICE WITH BEER ALLA VALDOSTANA
Risotto con birra, alla Valdostana

3 tablespoons butter
1 medium onion, sliced thin
1½ cups long-grain rice
1½ cups beer
2½ cups homemade or canned beef broth, heated
½ cup grated Parmesan cheese

Melt butter in a saucepan; add onion and cook over low heat until soft and golden. Add rice; stir and cook for 2 or 3 minutes. Add beer and cook until it has evaporated; add some hot broth; stir and cook gently at low heat; before it is all absorbed, add more broth and continue to cook until rice is tender, about 12 to 20 minutes; it should be creamy but firm. Transfer to a warm serving bowl; sprinkle with cheese and serve hot. Serves 6.

RICE WITH TRUFFLES ALLA PIEMONTESE
Risotto alla Piemontese con tartufi

One of the rarest, most expensive foods is the white truffle. The small town of Alba on the hills above Torino is the world's largest supplier of white truffles. A good specimen can cost up to fifty dollars for one ounce. If you feel expensive and you would like to taste the flavor that has defied description for hundreds of years, make *Risotto con tartufi*. It is certain to be a delicious experience. Unlike the *risotto alla Milanese*, *Risotto alla Piemontese* is prepared without sautéing the rice first. It is best made with rich homemade chicken broth.

  2   cups homemade chicken broth
  2   cups of water
1½   cups long-grain rice
  ½   cup the best grated Parmesan cheese you can find
  6   tablespoons butter, at room temperature
      pinch nutmeg
      salt to taste
  1   small truffle

In a saucepan, heat broth and water to boiling; add rice and stir frequently to prevent rice from sticking. When it looks creamy, neither dry nor runny, it is ready; this should take from 12 to 15 minutes. Turn off heat; add cheese, butter, and nutmeg; stir gently and add salt to taste. Spoon it into a heated serving bowl and cover the top with a layer of very thinly sliced truffle. Serve immediately. Serves 4 to 6.

RICE WITH BARBERA WINE
Risotto al Barbera

Barbera is fresh red wine typical of the vintages of the hills of Piemonte.

        2   tablespoons butter
        3   tablespoons oil
        1   small onion, sliced thin
     1½   cups long-grain rice
        2   cups Barbera (red) wine
        2   cups homemade or canned beef broth, heated

Melt butter in a skillet; add oil and onion; sauté until soft, about 5 minutes. Add rice and stir until well coated. Add wine; stir and cook over low heat until the wine is all absorbed. Add broth, a little at a time, and continue to cook until the rice is tender, about 15 to 20 minutes; it should be creamy but firm. Serves 6.

PASTA PREFERENCES

Cooking pasta, like many other things, is a matter of taste. The majority of Italian cookbooks tell you to cook pasta "al dente," until tender, but still firm. I, and many others, do not like pasta "al dente"; therefore I will not tell you that you must cook pasta until just firm. Cooking time varies with the type of pasta you use, fresh, homemade, dried, thick, or thin; after you have dropped the pasta into boiling salted water and the water has resumed boiling, do not cover; taste at intervals and cook the pasta to the texture that pleases you.

The easiest and tastiest pasta dishes one can prepare are sauced with simple herb butters. Sage, rosemary, bay leaves, chives, or marjoram can be used. It is preferable to use fresh herbs, but if fresh herbs are not available, use dried herbs. The ratio for fresh herbs is three times the amount of the dried varieties called for in these recipes. Please, do not use powdered herbs. My favorite pasta butter is seasoned with sage.

EGG NOODLES WITH SAGE
Tagliatelle alla salvia

¼ pound butter
1½ teaspoons dried sage leaves
1½ teaspoons salt
1 pound egg noodles
½ cup grated Parmesan cheese

In a small saucepan melt butter over low heat; add sage and simmer for 15 minutes. Heat 4 quarts of water to boiling. Add salt; drop in the noodles; stir and cook to your taste; try them after 5 minutes of cooking time. When done to your taste, drain and transfer to a warm serving bowl. Pour melted butter, through a strainer, over hot pasta; toss lightly; add cheese; toss rapidly and serve immediately. Serves 4 to 6.

HOMEMADE EGG NOODLES
Pasta all'uovo fatta in casa

Although factory-manufactured egg noodles are good, none can compare with the delicate texture and flavor of fresh, homemade pasta.

4 cups all-purpose flour
4 eggs
4 tablespoons milk
1½ teaspoons salt

Make a mound of flour on a pastry board with a well in the center. Break eggs into a bowl and beat with milk and salt; pour into center of flour well. Working with your fingers, mix flour into eggs a little at a time, until flour is used. You will then have a rough dough. Turn out on a floured surface and with both hands knead the dough with the heels of your hands, folding it over, slapping it down, folding it again and again for about 10 minutes, until dough is smooth and elastic. Form into a ball; cover it with a towel and let it rest for 15 minutes.

Divide dough into four pieces; cover pieces you are not using. Dust work surface with flour, and with a long rolling pin, roll pasta dough into a sheet about ⅛ of an inch thick. Transfer to a well-floured tablecloth and repeat operation with remaining dough. Do not let sheets of pasta dry for longer than 15 minutes. Taking one sheet of pasta at a time, roll it into a 3-inch flat roll and cut crosswise to desired width. For *tagliatelle,* or *fettuccine,* cut ¼-inch wide; for *tagliarini,* cut ⅛-inch wide; for *spaghetti,* cut ⅟₁₆-inch wide; for *pappardelle,* cut 1-inch wide.

When you have cut all rolls, unfold them; spread pasta over a dry towel to dry for at least 5 minutes before cooking.

To cook, drop into 7 or 8 quarts of salted, boiling water; cook for 2 minutes. Drain and serve with your favorite sauce, or one of mine. The recipe can be cut in half. Serves 8.

EGG NOODLES WITH SPINACH SAUCE
Pasta all'uovo con salsa di spinaci

This is a splendid sauce for either fresh or dried noodles.

1	pound fresh spinach or 1 10-ounce package frozen spinach, thawed
2	cloves garlic
6	sprigs fresh parsley
2	tablespoons pine-nuts
¼	cup oil
1½	teaspoons salt
¼	teaspoon white pepper
1	pound egg noodles
2	tablespoons butter or margarine
½	cup grated Parmesan cheese

Wash fresh spinach; drain fresh or frozen spinach. In electric blender, puree spinach, garlic, parsley, and pine-nuts. Pour mixture into a bowl; add salt and pepper; beat with a fork; set aside. Drop noodles into 4 quarts of boiling, salted water; stir and cook to your taste; start testing after 5 minutes of cooking time. When ready, drain, return to same kettle; add butter and half of spinach sauce; stir lightly until butter is melted and the noodles are well coated. Transfer to a warm serving bowl; spoon remaining sauce over. Top with cheese and serve immediately. Serves 4 to 6.

PASTA WITH EGG SAUCE ALL'ASTIGIANA
Pasta asciutta all'Astigiana

All'Astigiana means in the style of Asti, a city in the center of the hilly region of Piemonte.

1 pound spaghetti or noodles of your choice
6 tablespoons butter, at room temperature
4 egg yolks, well beaten
2 tablespoons chopped fresh parsley
½ teaspoon salt
¼ teaspoon white pepper
1 cup grated Parmesan cheese

Cook pasta to your taste; drain and transfer to a warm serving bowl. Add butter and toss to thoroughly coat pasta; add egg yolks and toss vigorously; mix in parsley, salt, pepper, and cheese. Toss and serve immediately. Serves 4 to 6.

EGG NOODLES WITH CAVIAR
Pasta all'uovo, con caviale

1 8-ounce package cream cheese, at room temperature
2 ounces caviar of your choice
2 egg yolks, at room temperature
4 tablespoons grated Parmesan cheese
1 pound egg noodles

In a bowl, combine cream cheese and caviar; blend well; add egg yolks, Parmesan cheese and mix to a smooth sauce. Cook noodles in salted water to your taste; drain and transfer to a warm serving bowl; add cheese-caviar sauce; toss and serve immediately. Serves 6.

PASTA BARDO-NECCHIA-STYLE
Pasta asciutta alla Bardonecchia

Bardonecchia is a lively frontier mountain town with Alpine roads rising to the eternal snows. Here one can ski even in the summertime. *Pasta asciutta* means any pasta of your choice, cooked, drained and served with a sauce.

4 tablespoons butter
4 tablespoons oil
2 medium onions, sliced thin
½ pound fresh mushrooms, thinly sliced
½ teaspoon juniper berries, crushed
2 beef-bouillon cubes, crushed
1 pound noodles or spaghetti
½ cup heavy cream
½ cup grated Parmesan cheese

In a skillet, melt butter; add oil and onions; cook over low heat until onions are golden; add mushrooms, juniper berries, and bouillon cubes; cook, uncovered over low heat for 15 minutes. Meanwhile, cook pasta to your taste, drain and transfer to a warm serving bowl. Add cream to sauce, stir and pour over pasta; sprinkle with cheese; toss and serve immediately. Serves 4 to 6.

EGG NOODLES WITH UNCOOKED TOMATO SAUCE
Pasta all'uovo con pomodoro crudo

1 pound fresh sun-ripened tomatoes, or 1 16-ounce can plum tomatoes with juice
2 tablespoons oil
1 small onion, cut into pieces
½ cup fresh basil leaves
1 clove garlic
1 teaspoon salt
⅛ teaspoon white pepper
1 pound egg noodles

Put 1 cup tomatoes with juice, oil, onion, basil leaves, garlic, salt and pepper into electric blender; blend at high speed until ingredients are puréed. Blend remaining tomatoes and add to mixture. Cook noodles to your taste; drain and transfer to a warm serving bowl; pour tomato sauce over noodles; toss and serve immediately. Serves 4 to 6.

BAKED ROYAL PASTA MARIUCCIA

Pasta reale al forno, Mariuccia

This is not a true pasta. *Pasta Reale* is the name for small baked "nuggets." In this recipe, they are filled with a delicious surprise.

Preheat oven to 425°F.

Pasta:
- 2 cups water
- 1 cup butter
- 2 cups flour
- ½ teaspoon salt
- 5 eggs

Filling:
- 4 tablespoons butter
- 10 chicken livers, cut up
- ½ pound boneless veal, cut into small pieces
- 1 whole chicken breast, skinned, boned, cut into small pieces
- ½ celery stalk, cut into small pieces
- ½ small onion, sliced
- ½ cup dry white wine
- 3 egg yolks
- ½ teaspoon salt
- ¼ teaspoon white pepper
- 1½ cups Béchamel sauce, recipe page 65.
- ½ cup grated Parmesan cheese

To make the pasta: In a saucepan, heat water with butter to boiling; add flour all at once; stir vigorously with a wooden spoon. Remove from heat and cool for 5 minutes; then, beat in salt and eggs, one at a time, beating well after each addition until batter is glossy and smooth. Using a pastry bag, or measuring ½ teaspoon of batter for each nugget, form small mounds, 1-inch apart, on a Teflon-coated baking sheet. Bake for 15 to 20 minutes, until nuggets are puffed and golden. Remove from baking sheet and cool on a rack. The nuggets will keep fresh for a few days in an air-tight can.

Filling: Melt butter in a small skillet; sauté chicken livers, veal, chicken breast for 10 minutes. Add celery, onion, and wine; cover and cook for 10 minutes over low heat. Remove from heat and chop mixture in electric blender. Add egg yolks, salt, and pepper to mixture. Make a small hole in each nugget, and with a pastry bag, using a small nozzle, fill nuggets with meat mixture. Arrange in layers in a buttered bake-and-serve dish; stir cheese into Béchamel sauce, and spoon over nuggets. Bake for 10 minutes. Serves 6.

SPINACH ROLL WITH BUTTER AND CHEESE
Rotolo di spinaci al burro e formaggio

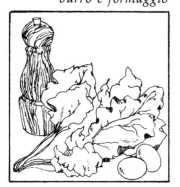

Preheat oven to 425°F.

Filling:
- 2 pounds fresh spinach, or 2 10-ounce packages frozen, chopped spinach
- 2 eggs, beaten
- 1 3-ounce package cream cheese
- 1 cup grated Parmesan cheese
- ½ teaspoon salt
- ¼ teaspoon black pepper
- 6 tablespoons butter

Dough:
- 2 cups all-purpose or whole-wheat flour
- 3 eggs, beaten
- 1 teaspoon salt

Clean, wash, and steam fresh spinach for 8 minutes; drain. Or steam frozen spinach for 8 to 10 minutes, drain. When spinach has cooled, squeeze out excess water; put in a bowl; stirring rapidly, combine spinach, eggs, cream cheese, ½ cup Parmesan cheese, salt, and pepper. Set aside. To make dough, put flour on a pastry board and shape it into a mound; make a well in the center and pour beaten eggs into well. Work with fingers into a soft dough. Roll dough into a 13 × 9-inch paper-thin sheet. Spread spinach filling over dough to 2 inches from edge; roll dough into a tubular shape; wrap tightly in cheesecloth; tie ends with string. In a large pot, heat 4 quarts of salted water to boiling; lower roll into kettle, reduce heat and boil gently for 20 minutes. Remove from water and cool. Meanwhile, heat butter and combine with remaining ½ cup Parmesan cheese. Unwrap roll, cut into 1-inch slices; arrange in a large shallow bake-and-serve dish, overlapping rolls slightly; pour butter-cheese sauce over; bake for 10 minutes. Serves 6 to 8.

LASAGNE ALLA GIOVANNI
Lasagne alla Giovanni

This is my brother Giovanni's special lasagne.

Preheat oven to 400°F.

8	tablespoons butter
1½	pounds fresh mushrooms, washed, thinly sliced
½	teaspoon salt
¼	teaspoon black pepper
½	cup dry white wine
1½	cups Béchamel sauce, page 65.
6	hard-cooked eggs, peeled and quartered
1	6-ounce can liver pâté with truffles
1	tablespoon brandy
1	pound lasagne
	grated Parmesan cheese
1	large fresh tomato, sliced

In a small saucepan melt 2 tablespoons butter; add mushrooms and sauté for 2 or 3 minutes; add ¼ teaspoon salt, pepper, and sprinkle with wine; lower heat and cook for 10 minutes; add mushroom mixture to Béchamel sauce. Slice eggs lengthwise, scoop out yolks; force yolks through sieve; add liver pâté, 2 tablespoons of softened butter, brandy, and remaining ¼ teaspoon salt and mix with a fork. Fill egg whites with egg-yolk mixture. In a large kettle, cook lasagne in 4 quarts boiling, salted water for 10 minutes. Drain, and lay flat to dry on a towel.

Butter a large shallow bake-and-serve dish; arrange 3 or 4 layers consisting of a portion each of mushrooms, lasagne, and cheese, saving enough cheese and sauce for the top. Garnish with stuffed eggs and tomato slices; dot with 2 tablespoons remaining butter, top with remaining sauce, and sprinkle with cheese. Bake for 20 minutes. Serves 6.

RAVIOLI ALLA TORINESE
Agnolotti alla Torinese

Agnolotti is the Torinese name for ravioli.

Preheat oven to 350°F.
Filling:
- 4 tablespoons butter
- 2 tablespoons oil
- ¼ teaspoon dried rosemary leaves, crumbled
- 2 pounds lean roasting beef
- 1 pound lean roasting pork
- 4 or 5 Savoy cabbage leaves
- 5 eggs, lightly beaten
- ½ teaspoon salt
- ¼ teaspoon black pepper
- ¼ teaspoon nutmeg
- 1 cup grated Parmesan cheese

Dough:
- 4 cups flour
- 4 eggs
- 2 teaspoons salt

Melt butter in a small roasting pan; add oil, rosemary, beef, and pork; cover and bake for 1 hour and 15 minutes; add cabbage leaves and bake 15 minutes longer. Remove from oven and cool for 15 minutes. Put meats and cabbage through food grinder. Put in a bowl, combine meats, eggs, salt, pepper, nutmeg, and ½ cup Parmesan cheese; mix well with a fork. Set aside. To make dough, mound flour on a pastry board; form a well in the center; add unbeaten eggs, and salt and mix with fingers until the dough is very smooth and stiff. Divide dough into 4 or 5 pieces; cover the pieces not immediately used with a damp towel; flour the board; with rolling pin, roll dough, one piece at a time, into a very thin sheet. Divide each sheet of dough in half; using a teaspoon, arrange filling in neat little mounds, 2 inches apart. Cover with other half of dough; press fingers on all unfilled spaces to seal. Cut with pastry wheel into 2-inch squares and sprinkle with flour. Cover with a dry towel. Cook *agnolotti* in a deep kettle of boiling, salted water for 5 minutes; drain with slotted spoon and transfer to a hot serving platter; spoon over some of your favorite sauce, or the Signor Antonio sauce, page 66. Serve at once with remaining ½ cup cheese in a separate bowl. Serves 12.

CAPPELLETTI "BELVEDERE"
Cappelletti alla "Belvedere"

The word *cappelletti* means little hats. The dough may be formed into priests' hats (di Prete) or clowns' hats (Cappelli di Pagliaccio).

3 tablespoons butter
3 thin slices Italian prosciutto, cut into strips
3 thin slices boiled ham, cut into strips
1 whole chicken breast, boned and cut into cubes
½ teaspoon salt
¼ teaspoon white pepper
½ teaspoon nutmeg
1½ pounds calves' brain
3 eggs
1 cup grated Parmesan cheese
Dough:
1 recipe for homemade noodles for 6, page 45.
8 cups homemade or canned beef broth
1 cup heavy cream
4 tablespoons butter
½ cup grated Parmesan cheese
1 small truffle, sliced very thin (optional)

Filling: Melt butter in a skillet; add prosciutto, ham, and chicken; cook gently over medium heat for 5 minutes. Stir occasionally to brown chicken lightly. Sprinkle with salt, pepper, and nutmeg; remove from heat and cool. Meanwhile, soak brain in cold water for 15 minutes, pull off and discard membranes and veins; rinse well. Simmer brain in 5 cups boiling, salted water, covered for 15 minutes. Drain and cool. Coarsely chop prosciutto, ham, and chicken; transfer to a bowl and combine with chopped brain, eggs and cheese. With a large fork mix thoroughly. Add salt to taste. Set aside.

Prepare dough as directed in recipe for Homemade Noodles, page 45. Divide the dough in three pieces, cover reserved pieces with a towel to prevent drying. Roll one piece at a time into a very thin sheet; cut into 2-inch rounds with a cookie cutter. Put a mound of filling on each round, about ¼ teaspoon; fold in half, making a half moon, wrap around your index finger, join the two ends together and press firmly, forming "little hats." Place on a clean towel in a single layer to prevent sticking. Continue until all the dough and filling have been used. Makes 200 to 250 *cappelletti*.

Heat the broth to boiling; drop in *cappelletti*. Freshly made *Cappelletti* will cook in 5 minutes; if they are dry, they will cook in 15 minutes. Meanwhile, in a small saucepan combine cream and butter; and simmer over low heat for 1 to 2 minutes, until thickened. Set aside. When done, transfer *cappelletti* with a slotted spoon to a warm serving platter. Pour cream-butter sauce over; stir gently to coat with sauce, sprinkle with cheese and truffle, and serve.

LASAGNE ALLA TORINESE
Lasagne alla Torinese

Preheat oven to 400°F.

2	ounces dried wild mushrooms
1	pound lasagne
6	tablespoons butter
1	pound chicken livers, cut in pieces
1	pound fresh mushrooms, sliced
3	tablespoons Meat-Base Sauce, page 67, or 3 beef-bouillon cubes
½	cup dry white wine
1	teaspoon salt
¼	teaspoon white pepper
1	cup grated Parmesan cheese

Soak mushrooms in enough warm water to cover for 30 minutes. Cook lasagne in 3 quarts boiling, salted water for 5 minutes; drain and lay flat on towels to dry. Wash wild mushrooms; drain and chop. Melt 4 tablespoons butter in a saucepan; add wild mushrooms, chicken livers, fresh mushrooms, Meat-Base Sauce, wine, salt and pepper; stir, cover and cook over low heat for 15 minutes. Butter a large shallow bake-and-serve dish; arrange in three or four layers with portions each of lasagne, chicken-liver-mushroom sauce, and cheese. Continue with two or three additional layers of lasagne, sauce, and cheese. Finish with a top layer of sauce, dots of remaining butter, and cheese. Bake for 20 minutes. Serves 6.

BAKED LASAGNE WITH CHICKEN
Lasagne al forno con pollo

Preheat oven to 400°F.

6	tablespoons butter
4	tablespoons flour
1	cup homemade or canned chicken broth, heated
½	cup milk, scalded
1½	teaspoons salt
¼	teaspoon white pepper
⅛	teaspoon nutmeg
1	teaspoon lemon juice
3	tablespoons oil
½	pound lasagne
1	cup cooked chicken, chopped
2	tablespoons unflavored bread crumbs

In a small saucepan, over low heat, melt 4 tablespoons butter; blend in flour; stir until golden; gradually add combined hot broth and milk; stir constantly until sauce begins to boil. Remove from heat; add ½ teaspoon salt, pepper, nutmeg, and lemon juice. Set aside. Heat 2 quarts water to boiling; add 1 teaspoon salt and oil; drop in lasagne and cook for 10 to 12 minutes; drain, and lay it flat on a towel to dry. Grease an 8-inch square bake-and-serve dish; arrange 3 or 4 layers with a portion each of lasagne, chicken, and sauce. Top with a final layer of lasagne and sauce. Sprinkle with bread crumbs and remaining 2 tablespoons of melted butter. Bake for 35 minutes and serve. Serves 4 to 6.

CREAM-OF-WHEAT DUMPLINGS
Gnocchi di semolino

Gnocchi is pronounced "Nunyah-kee" and means "dumplings."

Preheat oven to 425°F.
- 1 quart milk
- 1 cup cream of wheat (often called "farina")
- 2 egg yolks
- 1 cup grated Parmesan cheese
- 1 3-ounce package cream cheese
- 1 teaspoon salt
- ¼ teaspoon white pepper
- 6 tablespoons butter

In a saucepan, heat milk to boiling; lower the heat; add cream of wheat a little at a time, stirring constantly with a wooden spoon, until all has been added. Continue stirring and cook over very low heat for 10 minutes longer. Remove from heat; mixing rapidly, add egg yolks, ½ cup Parmesan cheese, cream cheese, salt, and pepper. Oil a flat surface; with spatula, spread cream of wheat to ½-inch thickness; let cool completely. Butter bottom of a large bake-and-serve dish; cut cream of wheat into rounds with a 2-inch glass or cookie cutter; arrange in baking dish slightly overlapping. Dot with butter and sprinkle with remaining ½ cup Parmesan cheese. Bake for 20 minutes. Serves 6.

POTATO DUMP-LINGS WITH FONTINA CHEESE
Gnocchi alla bava

Bava means dribble. In this recipe the gnocchi are dribbled with melted cheese.

Preheat over to 350°F.
- 1 recipe for potato dumplings, page 57, omit Parmesan cheese
- 1 pound Fontina cheese, slivered
- 4 tablespoons butter

Make dumplings as previously directed. Boil them; lift with slotted spoon and transfer to a buttered bake-and-serve dish; arrange in layers alternating with cheese, ending with a top layer of cheese; dot with butter. Cover loosely with foil and bake for 10 minutes. Serves 6 to 8.

POTATO DUMPLINGS ALLA PIEMONTESE
Gnocchi di patate alla Piemontese

Potato dumplings are good accompaniments for *Pollo alla Cacciatora "Belvedere,"* page 125. Unbuttered Potato Dumplings can also be served with Bagna Caôda, page 6, poured over, then tossed gently.

2 pounds baking potatoes
2 egg yolks
2 tablespoons olive oil
½ teaspoon grated nutmeg
1 to 1½ cups flour
6 tablespoons butter, melted
½ cup grated Parmesan cheese

Cook unpeeled potatoes in boiling salted water until tender, about 30 minutes. Drain, peel as soon as they are cool enough to handle, and put them through a potato ricer over a pastry board; add egg yolks, oil, and nutmeg; mix in flour, a little at a time, and knead into a smooth soft dough; roll into sausage-shaped long rolls the thickness of your finger; cut into 1-inch pieces. Hold a piece with a fork in your other hand, and press each piece down, rolling it gently with the fork prongs to make ridges in one side, while your thumb makes a deep depression in the other side. Cook dumplings in several batches, about 20 in a pot at once. Drop dumplings, one by one into gently boiling salted water; cook for 5 to 7 minutes. Lift them out with a slotted spoon as they rise to the surface; transfer to a warm serving bowl; dribble over some of the melted butter. When all are cooked, toss them very gently with the cheese, or omit butter and cheese and serve with your favorite sauce. Serves 6 to 8.

OATMEAL DUMPLINGS
Gnocchi di avena

2 pounds potatoes
1 pound fresh spinach or broccoli, or 1 10-ounce package frozen spinach or broccoli
1½ cups rolled oats (not quick-cooking)
½ pound Fontina or Gruyère cheese, diced
3 eggs
2 teaspoons salt
1 pound onions, sliced thin
3 tablespoons unflavored breadcrumbs
4 tablespoons butter

Wash, peel and finely grate potatoes; squeeze out excess liquid. Wash fresh spinach or broccoli, coarsely chop, and cook in boiling salted water for 5 minutes. If you are using a frozen vegetable, thaw and squeeze out all liquid. In a large bowl, combine potatoes, spinach or broccoli, oats, cheese, eggs, and salt; mix well with fingers. Cover and refrigerate for 1 hour. Using the palm of your hand, roll mixture into ¾-inch balls. Heat 4 quarts of salted water to boiling; drop in dumplings, a few at a time, and cook for 4 to 5 minutes. Drain with slotted spoon, and transfer to a large shallow bake-and-serve dish; arrange in layers alternating with onion slices; sprinkle each layer with breadcrumbs, dot with butter. Preheat broiler for 5 minutes; place dish 3 inches from heat and broil for 5 minutes. This dish can be prepared in advance and broiled just before serving. Serves 6 to 8.

POLENTA
Polenta

Polenta could be considered the bread of Northern Italy. People believe that polenta was originated when Cristoforo Colombo returned from America with corn; but history books tell us that the Roman army ate a corn-porridge dish with their meals. But, whatever the source, it is a delicious accompaniment for stewed dishes of meat, game, or fish. It is also good with fried fish and squids, or, by itself, dressed with butter and cheese. My ancestors cooked polenta for one to two hours in a copper "paiolo," or cauldron. Now, using a Teflon-lined deep pot, it can be ready to eat in 15 or 20 minutes.

5 cups water
2½ cups yellow cornmeal flour
1 tablespoon salt

In a small bowl combine 1 cup of cold water with cornmeal. Bring remaining 4 cups water with salt to a boil in a Teflon-coated saucepan; gradually stir in cornmeal mixture; cover tightly and simmer for 15 minutes. The polenta will leave the sides of pan when done. Unmold polenta onto a warm serving platter, and serve with butter and cheese or sauce of your choice. For a delicious breakfast treat, slice left-over polenta and toast both sides under broiler heat. Makes 6 to 8 servings.

POLENTA WITH MUSHROOMS
Polenta con funghi

Preheat oven to 425°F.
1 recipe of Polenta, page 58
1 ounce dried wild mushrooms
6 tablespoons butter
4 tablespoons flour
2 cups milk, heated
½ teaspoon salt
¼ teaspoon white pepper
⅛ teaspoon nutmeg
½ cup grated Parmesan cheese
1 pound fresh mushrooms

Prepare hot polenta as recipe directs; transfer to a wooden block; spread 2 inches thick and cool. Soak wild mushrooms in one cup of lukewarm water for 15 minutes. Meanwhile, in a small saucepan, melt 4 tablespoons of butter; blend in flour and cook for a few minutes, stirring constantly, with a wooden spoon. Remove from heat and add hot milk, a little at a time; continue stirring, over low heat, until sauce is creamy and smooth. Add salt, pepper, nutmeg, and cheese. Wash fresh mushrooms, pat dry, and cut in thin slices; cook for 5 minutes in a saucepan with remaining 2 tablespoons butter. Dry and chop wild mushrooms; add to fresh mushrooms; continue cooking for 5 minutes. In buttered 9-inch pie dish, arrange two or three triple layers of polenta slices, ½-inch thick, sauce, and mushrooms, finishing with a top layer of sauce. Bake for 15 minutes and serve hot. Serves 6.

POLENTA FOR THE WEALTHY TORINESE
Polenta ricca Torinese

This is a good make-ahead-and-bake-at-the-last-minute dish for V.I.P. company.

Preheat oven to 425°F.
recipe of polenta, page 58 (use 5 cups of milk in place of water)
- 1 pound Fontina cheese, cut into rounds ¼ inch thick and 2 inches in diameter
- ½ pound thinly sliced lean boiled ham, cut into 2-inch rounds
- 1 small truffle, sliced thin (this is the reason for the name of the recipe)
- 4 tablespoons butter

Spread freshly made hot polenta in ½-inch layer on a wooden board, cool. With a 2-inch glass or a cookie cutter, cut polenta into rounds. Cut cheese and ham into 2-inch rounds. Butter a large baking dish. Sandwich each round of polenta with cheese, ham, and a few slices of truffles. Top with another round of polenta. Arrange in buttered baking dish; dot with butter and bake for 15 minutes. Serves 6 to 8.

POLENTA ALLA VALDOSTANA
Polenta alla Valdostana

Preheat oven to 425°F.
- 1 recipe of Polenta, page 58. (Use 3 cups of milk and 2 cups of water.)
- 1 pound Fontina or Swiss cheese
- 6 tablespoons butter
- 4 tablespoons grated Parmesan cheese

Transfer hot freshly cooked polenta to a wooden block; spread and cool. In a buttered 9-inch pie dish arrange a series of layers of ½-inch polenta slices, cheese, and a few dots of butter. The top layer should be cheese. Dot with butter, sprinkle with Parmesan cheese and bake for 15 minutes. Serves 6.

TORINESE BREAD STICKS
Grissini

Preheat oven to 375°F. 10 minutes before baking
2 packages yeast
1 cup lukewarm milk
4 cups flour
warm water
¼ cup olive oil
1 teaspoon salt
2 tablespoons sugar

Soften yeast in lukewarm milk; stir in 2 cups flour and mix well. Add remaining flour alternately with enough warm water to make a dough. Add oil, salt and sugar, and turn out on a floured board; cover and allow dough to rest for 15 minutes, then knead until smooth, about 15 minutes. Transfer dough to a greased bowl; cover and let rise in a warm place, until double in size, about 1 hour. Turn out dough on a floured board and knead lightly for 5 minutes. Shape dough into 36 to 40 balls 2 inches in diameter. Roll out and stretch each ball with the palm of your hands until 8 to 10 inches long. Place on a floured board; cover with towel and let rise until double in size, about 30 to 40 minutes. Bake for 15 to 20 minutes, or until very light gold in color. Makes about 36 to 40 *grissini*.

FAT POLENTA

Polenta grassa

½ Polenta recipe, page 58
6 tablespoons butter
4 cloves garlic, finely chopped
6 tablespoons grated Parmesan cheese

Spoon hot freshly cooked polenta in little mounds in a buttered dish. Cover and keep warm. Melt butter in a small saucepan; add garlic; cover and cook over very low heat for 15 minutes. Spoon garlic butter over polenta; sprinkle with cheese and serve immediately. Serves 6.

4
Sauces

Salse

You will find in this chapter sauces that you know, like Mayonnaise, and Béchamel, but with variations. It is the Piemontese touch that makes them different. Also you will be surprised by the many sauces that are uniquely Piemontesi, like Bagna Caôda, a divine concoction that you will surely enjoy, as well as Bee's Sauce, Red Sauce, and Green Sauce, three exciting sauces for boiled meats or cold roast beef.

Brandy Sauce is yet another created especially to enhance seafood and fish. There are also delicious sauces for *fettuccine* and *agnolotti*. These owe their character to the use of herbs and spices.

ANCHOVY SALAD DRESSING
Bagna freida, per insalata

Freida is the Piemontese word for "cold."

4 anchovy fillets
1 clove garlic
⅓ cup oil
3 tablespoons wine vinegar
⅛ teaspoon black pepper
salt

Chop anchovies and garlic very fine; put in a small jar; add oil, vinegar, and pepper; shake thoroughly. Refrigerate. Before serving, add salt to taste. Shake and pour over torn lettuce, thinly sliced celery, or egg, potato, or seafood salads. Makes ½ cup.

BÉCHAMEL SAUCE OR WHITE SAUCE
Salsa Besciamella

4 tablespoons butter
1 small onion, quartered (optional)
4 tablespoons flour
2 cups milk
½ teaspoon salt
¼ teaspoon white pepper
⅛ teaspoon nutmeg

In a small saucepan over low heat, melt butter; add onion, sauté for a few minutes; discard onion. Add flour, stirring constantly until blended. In another saucepan, scald milk. Pour hot milk all at once into the butter-flour mixture and stir until thickened. Stir in salt, pepper, and nutmeg; simmer slowly, stirring constantly, for 10 minutes, and the sauce is ready for use. This is an all-purpose sauce. Makes 2 cups.

SAUCE FOR AGNOLOTTI SIGNOR ANTONIO
Salsa per agnolotti Signor Antonio

This sauce is also superb over *spaghetti*, *fettuccine* and with boiled rice.

2	ounces dried wild mushrooms
4	tablespoons butter
1	pound lean ground beef
½	cup dry white wine
1	medium onion, chopped
1	carrot, chopped
2	stalks celery, chopped
2	whole cloves garlic
2	tablespoons chopped fresh parsley
1	teaspoon salt
¼	teaspoon white pepper
⅛	teaspoon nutmeg
1	16-ounce can plum tomatoes
1	cup homemade or canned beef broth

Soak wild mushrooms in lukewarm water for ½ hour; drain, wash, and chop. In frying pan, melt butter, add and brown meat; add mushrooms and cook for 5 minutes; add wine and cook 5 minutes longer. With slotted spoon, remove meat and mushrooms. To juices remaining in pan, add onion, carrot, celery, garlic, parsley, salt, pepper, and nutmeg; cook for 15 to 20 minutes, until vegetables are soft. Add tomatoes with juice and beef broth; cover and simmer for 2 hours. Remove garlic cloves before serving. Makes 3 cups.

BRANDY SAUCE FOR FISH AND SHELLFISH
Salsa al cognac, per pesci e crostacei

3 hard-cooked egg yolks
1 tablespoon prepared Dijon mustard
¾ cup oil
2 tablespoons brandy
2 tablespoons dry white wine
salt and pepper to taste

Into electric blender on low speed, blend egg yolks and mustard; turn to a medium speed and gradually add oil, drop by drop, until mixture is very thick. Alternately continue adding oil, then brandy and wine. Remove from blender; add salt and pepper. Pour into a small jar or bowl; cover and refrigerate until serving time. Makes 1 cup.

MEAT BASE FOR SAUCES
Fumêt

4 tablespoons butter
3 large onions, diced
2 medium carrots, diced
3 stalks celery, diced
1 pound short ribs of beef
5 pounds beef bones
2 cups dry white wine
1 teaspoon dried thyme leaves, crumbled
3 bay leaves
2 cloves garlic, finely chopped
3 quarts water
½ teaspoon peppercorns
2 teaspoons salt

Melt butter in a large kettle; add onions, carrots, celery, and short ribs; cook over medium heat for 30 minutes, stirring occasionally; do not burn, just brown. Add beef bones, wine, thyme, bay leaves, garlic, water, peppercorns, and salt. Bring to a boil; lower heat and simmer for 3 hours. Cool and strain; remove bay leaves; pour into small jars and freeze. Use as a base to enrich other meat sauces. Makes 1½ quarts.

GREEN SAUCE FOR MEATS
Salsa verde

This pungent sauce is always served with *Bollito Misto*, mixed boiled meat. It is also very good spread on bread for a roast beef sandwich.

1   cup finely chopped fresh parsley
4   anchovy fillets, or 1 tablespoon anchovy paste
1   tablespoon finely chopped onion
1   clove garlic, finely chopped
½   cup oil
3   tablespoons vinegar
1   hard-cooked egg yolk, mashed
½   teaspoon white pepper
salt to taste

Put all ingredients except salt in a bowl or jar and mix thoroughly; add salt to taste. Covered tightly, this sauce can be held in refrigerator for two weeks or more. Serve at room temperature with boiled meats. Makes 1¼ cups.

TOMATO PASTE OR RED SAUCE
Bagnet 'd tomatiche, salsina di pomodoro

This is an entirely different sauce for cooked meats, and cold meat sandwiches.

6   tablespoons tomato paste
1   teaspoon sugar
½   teaspoon salt
1   clove garlic, finely chopped
1½   teaspoons Dijon mustard
1   cup oil
¼   cup wine vinegar

Put all ingredients in a bowl or jar; mix thoroughly. Serve at room temperature. Covered tightly, this sauce will keep in the refrigerator for two weeks or more. Makes 1½ cups.

GREEN MAYONNAISE SAUCE
Salsa maionese verde

1 cup Mayonnaise Sauce, recipe below
1 small onion, finely chopped
1 tablespoon chopped fresh parsley
1 tablespoon chopped fresh tarragon
1 teaspoon chopped capers

In container of electric blender, put mayonnaise and all other ingredients; blend smooth. Makes 1¼ cups.

BEE'S SAUCE
Salsa delle api

Bee's sauce was popular in the middle ages. It has passed the test of ages, and is still much in evidence on Piemontese tables as an accompaniment for meats.

30 walnut halves
 1 cup honey
 2 tablespoons Dijon mustard
 2 tablespoons beef broth

Finely chop walnuts in electric blender. Thoroughly mix nuts and remaining ingredients in a bowl or jar. Refrigerate for 2 or 3 hours before serving. Makes 1½ cups.

MAYONNAISE SAUCE
Salsa maionese

For success with this recipe, all the ingredients should be at room temperature. If the mayonnaise *impazzisce*—goes crazy—that means oil and eggs separate, it is very simple to save it. Begin again with 1 egg yolk, and, instead of oil, add very slowly the "crazy" mayonnaise, beating constantly.

3 egg yolks
3 cups oil
juice of three lemons, strained
1 teaspoon salt
½ teaspoon white pepper

With a wire whisk, whip egg yolks in a bowl. Pour oil very slowly, drop by drop, beating constantly. After incorporating all the oil, very slowly add strained lemon juice, salt and pepper. Makes 3 cups.

5
Fish

Pesci

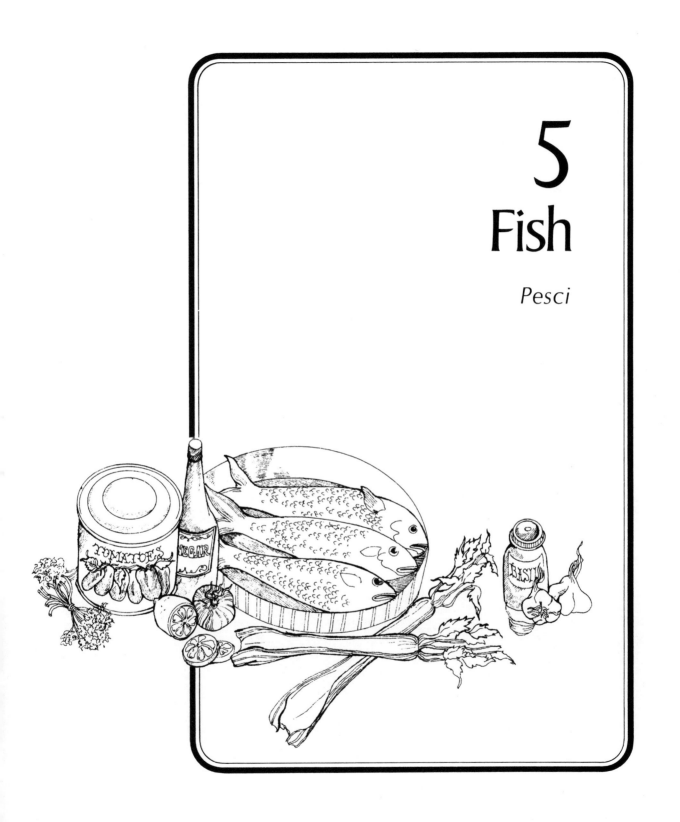

The Alpine streams of the Piemonte Valley provide beautiful trout. The upper Po Valley flashes with sparkling lakes and tributary rivers which supply freshwater perch, sunfish, carp, and bass. The rice fields are the habitat of frogs, tench, and eels. This abundance is prepared for the table by frying, stewing, marinating, and is often artistically arranged in aspic dishes.

TROUT WITH BAROLO ALLA TORINESE
Trote al Barolo, alla Torinese

Barolo is a full-bodied red wine from Piemonte.

Preheat oven to 350°F.

6	tablespoons butter
2	medium onions, sliced
1	celery stalk, diced
3	bay leaves
½	teaspoon dried thyme leaves, crumbled
4	sprigs of fresh parsley
4	8-ounce trout
1	24-ounce bottle Barolo wine
1	beef-bouillon cube, crushed
1	tablespoon flour
½	teaspoon salt
¼	teaspoon black pepper

Melt 3 tablespoons of butter in a baking pan; distribute onion, celery, bay leaves, thyme, parsley over butter; place trout on top of vegetables; cook over medium heat until vegetables are soft. Add wine, bouillon cube; heat to boiling. Remove to oven. Bake for 20 to 25 minutes, uncovered, basting every 10 minutes with juices in pan, until fish flakes easily with a fork and is just tender. Do not overcook. Transfer trout to a heated serving platter and keep warm. Force vegetables and juices through a sieve into a small saucepan; add crushed bouillon cube, remaining 3 tablespoons butter; blend in flour; heat to boiling, and cook for 2 minutes, stirring constantly. Remove from heat; add salt and pepper; pour over trout and serve. Serves 4.

TROUT WITH WHITE WINE SAUCE ALLA PIEMONTESE
Trote al vino bianco, alla Piemontese

6   8-ounce trout
¼   cup flour
6   tablespoons butter
1   teaspoon salt
¼   teaspoon white pepper
½   cup dry white wine
1   lemon, cut into wedges

Wash trout and pat dry with paper towels. Open flat; sprinkle with salt and pepper; coat with flour, shake off any excess. Heat 3 tablespoons butter in a large frying pan; place three trout, open side down, and cook 3 to 4 minutes, or until golden. Turn trout and cook 5 minutes longer. Transfer to a warm serving platter and keep warm while remaining trout are cooked. When all trout are done, scrape residue loose from the pan; add wine; cook uncovered, stirring over medium heat for 5 minutes. Spoon sauce over trout and serve with lemon wedges. Serves 6.

FILLET OF SOLE WITH AROMATIC SAUCE
Filetti di sogliola, con salsa aromatica

Marinade:
1   cup dry white wine
½   cup white vinegar
1   small onion, chopped
1   tablespoon chopped fresh parsley
1   teaspoon salt
¼   teaspoon white pepper
2   pounds fillets of sole or other white fish
oil for frying

In a small bowl combine wine, vinegar, onion, parsley, salt, and pepper; mix well. Arrange fish in a deep dish; pour marinade over and let stand at room temperature for 1 hour.

Sauce:
```
1   tablespoon butter
2   tablespoons oil
1   stalk celery, finely chopped
1   small onion, finely chopped
1   clove garlic, minced
1   8-ounce can plum tomatoes
1   tablespoon chopped fresh basil
½   cup dry white wine
½   teaspoon salt
¼   teaspoon black pepper
```

Melt butter in a small saucepan; add oil, celery, onion, and garlic; cook about 5 minutes, until onion and celery are soft. Add tomatoes and juice, basil, wine, salt, and pepper; bring to a boil, lower heat, cover and simmer for 1 hour.

Batter:
```
1   cup flour
⅛   teaspoon salt
2   tablespoons butter, melted
2   eggs, beaten
½   cup beer
oil for deep frying
```

Mix flour and salt in a bowl; stir in butter, and eggs; gradually stir in beer. Continue stirring until batter is smooth. Set aside in a warm place for 30 minutes. Heat oil in a frying pan. Dip each fillet in batter and fry for 2 or 3 minutes, until golden. Drain on paper towels; transfer to a warm serving dish. Serve hot with sauce in a separate dish. Serves 6.

GOLDEN FILLETS OF PERCH
Filetti di pesce persico, dorati

3	pounds fillets of perch
½	cup flour
3	eggs, well beaten
¾	cup butter
½	teaspoon salt
¼	teaspoon white pepper
1	lemon, cut in wedges

Wash fillets; pat dry with paper towels. Dip both sides of fillets in the flour; shake off excess; dip in beaten eggs. Heat butter in a large frying pan; cook fillets, a few at a time, until golden on both sides. Transfer to a heated serving dish; sprinkle with salt and pepper. Serve with lemon wedges. Serves 6.

FISH IN ASPIC
Pesce in gelatina

2	pounds fresh mullets, tench, sardines, or mackerel
	oil for frying
2	cups white vinegar
2	cups water
2	large onions, cut into thick slices
1	carrot, cut into 2-inch pieces
1	stalk celery, cut into 2-inch pieces
5	bay leaves
3	cloves garlic
3	cloves
1	teaspoon salt
½	teaspoon white pepper
2	egg whites, beaten
4	envelopes unflavored gelatine

Wash fish and dry with paper towels; heat 1 inch oil in a frying pan; fry fish until golden on both sides. Drain on paper towels and cool. In a saucepan, combine vinegar, water, onion, carrot, celery, bay leaves, garlic, cloves, salt, pepper, egg whites, and gelatine. Heat slowly, stirring constantly, until mixture comes to a boil; simmer for 5 minutes. Remove from heat, strain through several layers of cheesecloth and cool. Arrange fish in a deep bowl; pour cold gelatine over, and refrigerate for 48 hours before using. Fish in Aspic will keep in refrigerator up to two weeks. Serves 6 to 8.

FRESH CODFISH STEW
Merluzzo fresco in umido

2	tablespoons butter
3	tablespoons oil
1	large onion, chopped
1	clove garlic, chopped
3	tablespoons chopped fresh parsley
1	16-ounce can plum tomatoes, chopped
½	cup white vinegar
½	teaspoon salt
½	teaspoon white pepper
2	pounds fresh cod, or halibut

Melt butter in a large skillet; add oil, onion, and garlic; cook until onion is soft and golden. Stir in parsley, tomatoes with juice, vinegar, salt, and pepper. Cook covered, over low heat for 10 minutes. Wash fish; pat dry with paper towels; cut into serving pieces; add to sauce in skillet; heat to boiling; lower heat; cover and simmer for 45 minutes, until flesh leaves backbone easily when tested with a fork. Do not overcook. Check seasonings and serve hot, with Polenta; see recipe page 58. Serves 4 to 6.

MARINATED FISH
Pesci sott'aceto

2	pounds of smelts, tench, mackerel, or fresh sardines
	oil for frying
	salt
	pepper
1	medium onion, sliced
1	stalk celery, cut into 1-inch pieces
2	cloves garlic
2	whole cloves
3	cups white vinegar
1	cup dry white wine

In large skillet, in 1½ inches of hot oil, fry fish until golden. Drain on paper towels. Arrange in a deep dish, sprinkle with salt and pepper. For the marinade, heat ½ cup of oil used in frying, sauté onion, celery, garlic, and cloves until onion begins to turn golden. Add vinegar and wine; simmer, covered, for 30 minutes. Pour hot marinade over fish. Cover and refrigerate for 48 hours before serving. Marinated fish will keep in the refrigerator for 2 to 3 weeks. Serves 6.

FRIED FROGS' LEGS NOVARO-STYLE
Gambe di rane fritte alla Novarese

The rice-growing region of Piemonte is the home of well-fed frogs. The Novarese marinate the legs in a flavorful sauce, then fry them to crusty succulence. You might consider serving them as an unusual appetizer for a cocktail party.

2	cups water
2	cups vinegar
3	cloves garlic, whole
3	bay leaves
1	large onion
3	cloves
1	teaspoon salt
2	pounds frozen or fresh frogs' legs
½	cup flour
2	eggs, beaten
2	cups cornmeal flour
1	cup oil
½	teaspoon salt

In a saucepan, combine water, vinegar, garlic, bay leaves, onion, cloves, and salt; heat to boiling; lower heat and simmer for 15 minutes. Remove from heat and cool. Defrost frozen frogs' legs, wash and place in a bowl; pour over marinade and set aside at room temperature for 3 hours. Drain and dry; dredge in flour; dip in eggs, and then coat with cornmeal. Refrigerate for 30 minutes. Heat oil in a large skillet; drop frogs' legs into oil and cook 3 minutes on each side, until golden. Set aside on a paper towel to drain and keep warm until all are cooked. Sprinkle with salt and serve hot. Two pounds frogs' legs will serve 10 to 12.

FRIED SNAILS
Lumache fritte

This recipe is also good as a hot appetizer.

3   dozen canned snails, without shells
½   cup flour
2   eggs, beaten
½   cup cornmeal flour
oil for frying

Wash and dry snails; dredge in flour; dip in eggs, then coat with cornmeal flour. Refrigerate for 30 minutes. Heat oil in a skillet large enough to fry snails all at once; drop snails in hot oil and fry for 2 or 3 minutes, until golden. Drain on paper towels and serve warm on toothpicks. Serves 6.

SNAILS PIEMONTESE-STYLE
Lumache alla Piemontese

Fresh snails of good quality are not readily available here, so I prefer to use the canned variety; unfortunately they are expensive, and I must still my appetite for these delectable morsels. This recipe serves six as an appetizer course.

3   dozen canned snails, without shells
6   tablespoons butter
3   cloves garlic, chopped
2   tablespoons chopped fresh parsley
1   tablespoon chopped fresh basil
¼   pound chicken livers, chopped
3   hard-cooked egg yolks, chopped
½   cup dry white wine
2   tablespoons flour
¼   teaspoon salt
⅛   teaspoon black pepper
6   slices white bread, crusts removed, toasted

Wash snails and set aside. In a large saucepan, melt butter; add garlic, parsley, basil, chicken livers, and egg yolks; stir gently and cook for 10 minutes over low heat. Stir in wine, flour, snails, salt, and pepper. Cover and simmer for 15 minutes. Serve snails and sauce over slices of toasted bread. Serves 6.

6
Meats

Beef, Veal, Pork, Lamb, Variety Meats
Bue, Vitello, Maiale,
Agnello, Fuattaglie

Milk-fed calves of Piemonte, the Sanato, are rated the best in Italy. They give added cause for cheering the "Arte Culinaria" of this delightful region. True veal is from animals from four to fourteen weeks of age. They are most abundant in the late winter and spring. During the rest of the year, most of the meat sold in the United States as veal is actually calf.

In my experience, a carefully selected piece of beef tenderloin or eye-round can be substituted in many recipes for veal. Time after time, I have achieved equally delicious results with an economical substitute.

Latecomers to broaden the field of veal substitutes are chicken-breast and turkey-breast cutlets. They are excellent alternates for quick-cooking scaloppine and other briefly and gently cooked dishes.

Pork, lamb and variety meats are also treated to the high culinary standards of Piemonte. Again, wine and herbs develop the best in flavor and tenderness.

BEEF AND VEAL
Bue a Vitello

ROAST BEEF, ALLA VALDOSTANA
Arrosto di bue alla Valdostana

Preheat oven to 450°F.

6	pounds eye-round or rump of beef
2	large onions, sliced
3	cloves garlic, minced
2	bay leaves
1	teaspoon dried thyme leaves, crumbled
1	teaspoon juniper berries, crushed
6	sprigs fresh parsley
1	teaspoon salt
½	teaspoon black pepper
2	cups dry red wine, Barolo or Burgundy
6	tablespoons butter
1	cup homemade or canned beef broth
2	tablespoons flour

Put meat in a large bowl; add onions, garlic, bay leaves, thyme, juniper berries, parsley, salt, pepper, and wine. Cover bowl tightly and marinate for 24 hours in the refrigerator; stir a few times. Remove meat from marinade; pat dry. Strain marinade; reserve liquid and vegetables. Place meat on rack of a roasting pan. Roast for 30 minutes, basting twice with 4 tablespoons of melted butter. Reduce heat to 400°F.; add marinated vegetables and cook for 45 minutes, basting occasionally with fat from the pan. Transfer meat to a warm serving platter; let stand 15 minutes before slicing. Discard fat from pan; add marinade; bring to a boil and cook down to one half cup. Add broth; blend in remaining 2 tablespoons butter; add flour, stir until sauce is thick but smooth; strain. Slice meat and transfer to a warm platter. Serve sauce separately. Serves 8 to 12.

BRAISED BEEF WITH BAROLO
*Brasato di bue
al Barolo*

Preheat oven to 325°F.

1	4- to 5-pound beef round or rump roast
2	carrots, cut into 1-inch pieces
2	medium onions, sliced
3	bay leaves
2	cloves garlic
2	whole cloves
½	teaspoon rosemary leaves, crumbled
1	teaspoon salt
¼	teaspoon black pepper
3	cups Barolo wine, or Burgundy

Place meat in a large bowl; add carrots, onions, bay leaves, garlic, cloves, rosemary leaves, salt, and pepper; pour over wine. Cover and marinate in refrigerator for 24 hours, turning meat 3 or 4 times. Place meat, vegetables, and marinade in a Dutch oven. Cover and bake for 3 to 4 hours or until the meat is tender. Transfer meat to a warm serving platter and keep hot. Purée vegetables and pan juices through a food mill or in electric blender; if sauce is too thin, place over high heat and cook until it thickens. Slice meat, and pour some sauce over. Serve remaining sauce in separate dish, with another dish of mashed potatoes. Serves 8 to 10.

ROAST BEEF SALAD
Insalata di arrosto di bue avanzato

This hearty salad is usually made with leftover roast beef.

2 pounds roast beef, cooked, cooled, and cubed
1 large mild red onion, thinly sliced
1 green pepper, cubed
1 red pepper, cubed
2 large fresh tomatoes, cut into wedges
1 cup pitted olives
½ cup chopped fresh parsley
1 2-ounce can anchovy fillets, cut into 1-inch pieces
3 hard-cooked eggs, cut into wedges
9 tablespoons oil
3 tablespoons wine vinegar
1 clove garlic, minced
1 teaspoon Dijon mustard
1 teaspoon salt
½ teaspoon black pepper

Combine meat, onion, green and red pepper, tomatoes, olives, parsley, anchovy fillets, and eggs; sprinkle with a combination of oil, vinegar, garlic, mustard, salt, and pepper; toss well. Cover and refrigerate for 2 or 3 hours before serving. Serves 6 to 8.

BRAISED BEEF WITH MILK SIGNOR ANTONIO
Brasato di bue al latte, Signor Antonio

Pork loin, with some of the fat removed, can be braised in the same manner with delicious results.

½ cup flour
1 teaspoon salt
½ teaspoon black pepper
1 4- to 5-pound beef round or rump roast
6 strips bacon, chopped, or 4 thin slices Italian prosciutto, chopped
6 tablespoons butter
3 cups milk, heated
1 tablespoon flour

Mix flour, salt, and pepper, coat meat with mixture. Place bacon in a Dutch oven; add 4 tablespoons of butter and meat; brown meat on all sides. Add 1 cup of hot milk; cover tightly and simmer for 2 to 2½ hours, until meat is fork tender, basting it occasionally with remaining hot milk. When meat is done, transfer to a warm serving platter. Scrape cooking residue from pan; stir in remaining 2 tablespoons butter and flour. Stir until sauce thickens; pour into a serving bowl and serve with sliced meat. Serves 6 to 8.

APPETIZING POT ROAST
Stracotto appetitoso

2   tablespoons butter
4   tablespoons oil
1   3- to 4-pound beef chuck pot roast
1   large onion, chopped
2   carrots, chopped
2   stalks celery, chopped
1   whole clove garlic
2   bay leaves
½   teaspoon dried rosemary leaves, crumbled
½   teaspoon salt
½   teaspoon black pepper
1   cup dry white or red wine
2   beef-bouillon cubes
2   cups homemade or canned beef broth, heated

In a large Dutch oven, melt butter; add oil; over medium-high heat, brown meat on all sides. Lower heat; add onions, carrots, celery, and garlic; cook for 5 minutes, until onions are golden. Add bay and rosemary leaves, salt, pepper, wine, and bouillon cubes dissolved in 1 cup of broth. Cover and cook over medium-low heat for 2 to 3 hours; stir occasionally; as necessary add more broth. Transfer meat to a warm serving platter; force vegetables and liquids through a strainer and serve separately. Serves 6 to 8.

STUFFED BEEF ROLL
Arrosto ripieno

Preheat oven to 325°F.

1 2½- to 3-pound flank steak
1 large onion, chopped
1 tablespoon chopped fresh parsley
1 teaspoon dried marjoram, crumbled
½ pound lean ground beef
2 eggs, slightly beaten
1 teaspoon salt
½ teaspoon black pepper
3 hard-cooked eggs
¼ cup flour
2 tablespoons butter
2 tablespoons oil
½ cup dry red or white wine
½ cup water
1 beef-bouillon cube, crushed

With a sharp knife trim excess fat from steak. Score surface, one side only, ⅛-inch deep in a diamond pattern. Pound steak to flatten. In a bowl, thoroughly mix onion, parsley, marjoram, ground beef, beaten eggs, salt, and pepper. Spread stuffing over uncut side of steak; arrange whole hard-cooked eggs across center; roll up steak; tie securely with string and roll in flour. Melt butter in a roasting pan; add oil and brown rolled steak on all sides. Add wine, water, and bouillon cube. Cover and roast in oven for 2½ hours, turning roll several times during cooking. Transfer to a warm serving platter; remove string and keep warm. Loosen residue from sides and bottom of pan; reduce liquid to a thick sauce over high heat. Slice roll and pour sauce over. Serves 6.

BRAISED BEEF COOKED IN BEER
Carbonada alla Valdostana

The real "carbonada" is a salt-preserved beef found only in the Aosta Valley. Many years ago, when cattle herders, scattered high in the mountains, had no way of preserving the meat of a cow, slaughtered because of injury, they developed a method of preserving the meat with salt and pressure. Experimenting in my own way, I have originated a finished dish that tastes quite similar.

Preheat oven to 350°F.

- 3 cups beer
- 1 cup oil
- ½ cup vinegar
- 1 teaspoon salt
- 1 teaspoon black pepper
- 2 large onions, quartered
- 2 cloves garlic, crushed
- 5 pounds beef chuck pot roast
- ½ cup flour

In a large bowl, combine beer, ½ cup oil, vinegar, ½ teaspoon salt, ½ teaspoon pepper, onions, and garlic. Place meat in marinade; cover tightly; refrigerate overnight, turning meat two or three times. Drain meat, reserving marinade. Combine flour with remaining ½ teaspoon each salt and pepper. Heat remaining ½ cup oil in a roasting pan; pat meat dry with paper towels and rub with seasoned flour. In pan, brown meat over medium heat; add marinade; bring to a boil. Remove from stove; cover, and roast in oven for 2½ hours, turning meat occasionally and basting with pan liquids. When meat is done, slice it and transfer to a warm serving platter. Scrape residue from sides and bottom of pan; thicken liquid over high heat. Pour sauce over meat and serve immediately. Serves 6 to 8.

SCALOPPINE WITH MARSALA WINE "BELVEDERE"
Scaloppine al Marsala "Belvedere"

- 1 pound veal or beef tenderloin, cut ¼-inch thick
- ⅓ cup flour
- ¼ teaspoon salt
- ⅛ teaspoon white pepper
- 8 tablespoons butter
- ½ cup dry Marsala wine
- ¼ cup canned beef broth

Place each scaloppina between two pieces of waxed paper and pound thin. Dip each slice, on both sides, into the mixture of flour, salt, and pepper; shake off excess. Heat butter in a large frying pan over high heat, and brown scaloppine for 2 minutes on each side. Transfer to a warm serving platter; add Marsala and broth to juices in pan; stir and cook over high heat until reduced to half. Pour over meat and serve. Serves 4.

SCALOPPINE WITH PEAS

Scaloppine con piselli

The singular of scaloppine is scaloppina, as you will note in the following recipes.

1½ pounds veal or beef tenderloin, cut ¼-inch thick
½ teaspoon salt
1 cup flour
4 tablespoons butter
4 tablespoons oil
2 pounds unshelled peas, or 1 10-ounce package frozen peas, thawed
½ cup dry Marsala wine
1 beef-bouillon cube, crushed
½ cup hot water
1 tablespoon flour

Cut each scaloppina in half; pound it flat between two pieces of waxed paper; season with salt. Dip each scaloppina in flour on both sides; shake off excess. Over medium heat melt butter in a large skillet; add oil and sauté scaloppine, a few at a time, for 2 minutes on each side; transfer to a warm serving dish and keep warm. In same skillet, with fat remaining, cook frozen peas for 5 minutes, or fresh peas for 10 minutes. Add Marsala and bouillon cube dissolved in water; stir in flour; cook and stir over high heat for 2 minutes. Return scaloppine to the skillet for 2 minutes to reheat. Add salt to taste. Serve hot. Serves 6.

BREADED SCALOPPINE ALLA PIEMONTESE
Scaloppine panate, alla Piemontese

1½	pounds beef round, or scaloppine-style veal, ¼-inch thick, pounded thin
1	cup milk
2	eggs, beaten
1½	cups unflavored bread crumbs
4	tablespoons butter
½	teaspoon salt
¼	teaspoon white pepper
1	lemon, cut in wedges

Place meat in a bowl; pour milk over and set aside for 1 hour. Drain and pat dry with paper towels. Dip each slice into beaten eggs, and then into bread crumbs; coat well on both sides; shake off excess. Heat butter over medium heat in a large skillet; cook scaloppine in a large skillet without crowding, in several batches, browning slightly on both sides; drain on paper towels. Transfer scaloppine to a warm serving platter; sprinkle with salt and pepper. Serve with lemon wedges. Serves 6.

SCALOPPINE WITH HAM AND CHEESE
Scaloppine con prosciutto cotto e Fontina

12	scaloppine veal or beef tenderloin, ¼-inch thick, about 2 to 2½ pounds
½	teaspoon salt
¼	teaspoon white pepper
6	thin slices Italian prosciutto
6	thin slices Fontina cheese
⅔	cup flour
2	eggs, beaten
1½	cup unflavored bread crumbs
6	tablespoons butter
4	tablespoons oil
1	lemon, cut in wedges

Place each scaloppina between two pieces of wax paper and pound thin. Season with salt and pepper. Place a slice each of prosciutto and cheese on each of six scaloppine; top each with another scaloppina; press lightly together. Dip in flour on both sides; shake off excess; dip in eggs, then dredge in bread crumbs; pat with your hand and shake off any excess. Refrigerate for 1 hour. Melt butter in a large skillet over medium-low heat; add oil and cook a few scaloppine at a time, for 5 minutes on each side. Transfer to a warm serving dish; garnish with lemon wedges and serve immediately. Serves 6.

SCALOPPINE WITH TRUFFLE
Scaloppine al tartufo

6 scaloppine, veal or beef round, ¼-inch thick; do not pound
⅓ cup flour
½ teaspoon salt
6 tablespoons butter
1 small truffle, sliced thin (optional)
4 tablespoons grated Parmesan cheese
½ cup dry Marsala wine

Dip scaloppine in flour combined with salt; shake off excess. In a large skillet, melt butter and sauté scaloppine at high heat for 1 minute on each side. Transfer to a 9 × 9-inch bake-and-serve dish; place on top of each scaloppina a few slices of truffle; sprinkle with cheese. Put under preheated broiler for 2 or 3 minutes, or until cheese has melted. Loosen residue from bottom and sides of skillet; add Marsala; return to high heat; stir and cook for 2 or 3 minutes, until sauce thickens; pour gently over scaloppine and serve. Serves 4 to 6.

SCALOPPINE WITH ANCHOVIES
Scaloppine all'acciuga

6 scaloppine, veal or beef leg round, ¼-inch thick; do not pound
½ teaspoon salt
¼ teaspoon white pepper
⅓ cup flour
8 tablespoons butter
12 anchovy fillets, cut in half
3 tablespoons chopped fresh parsley
½ cup dry vermouth
1 lemon, cut into wedges

This time you do not pound the scaloppine, but cut each in half and season with salt and pepper. Dip lightly in flour; shake off excess. In a large skillet melt 6 tablespoons butter, and sauté scaloppine at high heat for 1 minute on each side. Transfer to a large bake-and-serve dish; place two pieces of anchovy on each scallopina; sprinkle with parsley, and dot with 2 tablespoons remaining butter. Put under preheated broiler for 2 or 3 minutes, or until butter is melted. Transfer scaloppine to a warm serving dish; loosen residue from bottom and sides of skillet; add vermouth; return to high heat; stir and cook for a few minutes, until sauce thickens. Pour over scaloppine and serve with lemon wedges. Serves 4 to 6.

SAUTÉED SCALOPPINE WITH TOMATO
Scaloppine con salsa di pomodoro

12	scaloppine veal or beef tenderloin, ¼-inch thick, about 2 to 2½ pounds
½	teaspoon salt
¼	teaspoon white pepper
1	cup flour
6	tablespoons butter
1	medium onion, finely chopped
1	8-ounce can plum tomatoes, drained and chopped
3	fresh basil leaves
½	cup dry vermouth

Place each scaloppina between two pieces of waxed paper and pound thin. Cut slices in half. Season with salt and pepper. Dip in flour on both sides; shake off excess. Melt butter in a large skillet over medium-high heat; sauté scaloppine 2 minutes on each side in several batches to prevent crowding; transfer to a warm serving dish; cover and keep warm. Add onion to butter in skillet; sauté until golden; add tomatoes and basil; lower heat and cook for 10 minutes; add vermouth and simmer 10 minutes longer. Remove basil leaves. Pour sauce over scaloppine and serve immediately. Serves 6.

STUFFED VEAL CHOPS ALLA PIEMONTESE
Costolette ripiene, alla Piemontese

Here is a very good way to use the last of the roast beef, turkey, or chicken.

 1 cup cooked meat, fine chopped
 3 eggs
 ½ cup grated Parmesan cheese
 2 tablespoons chopped fresh parsley
 6 veal chops with bone, about 1-inch thick, with pockets
 1½ cups unflavored bread crumbs
 6 tablespoons butter
 ½ teaspoon salt

In a bowl combine cooked meat, one egg, cheese, and parsley; stuff each chop with two tablespoons of meat mixture and close openings with toothpicks. Beat two remaining eggs; dip chops into eggs, then dredge in bread crumbs, pressing crumbs with your hand on both sides. Melt butter in a large skillet over medium heat and cook chops 5 minutes on each side. Sprinkle with salt. Transfer to a warm platter and serve immediately. Serves 6.

MARINATED STEAKS "BELVEDERE"
Bistecche sott'aceto, "Belvedere"

 6 slices veal or beef tenderloin, cut ¼-inch thick (do not pound)
 ¼ cup flour
 2 eggs, beaten, with 1 teaspoon salt
 ¾ cup unflavored bread crumbs
 6 tablespoons butter
 2 large onions, sliced thin
 6 sage leaves
 1 cup white-wine vinegar
 1 cup homemade or canned beef broth

Dip meat slices, on both sides, into flour. Shake off excess; dip slices into eggs and then into bread crumbs. Pat, and again shake off excess. Heat butter in a large frying pan; over medium heat, brown meat lightly on both sides. Remove from pan; drain on paper towels; set aside in a deep bowl. In same frying pan, cook onions with sage over low heat until onions are golden; skim off remaining fat; add vinegar and broth. Heat to boiling; lower heat and simmer for 15 minutes. Pour hot marinade over meat. Cool, cover and refrigerate for 24 hours before serving. Serve at room temperature. Marinated steaks will keep in refrigerator for one week. Serves 6.

VITELLO TONNATO "BELVEDERE"
Vitello Tonnato "Belvedere"

Here is the "Belvedere's" delectable version of one of the most individual of Italian recipes. It is a beautiful dish to serve as an appetizer for a formal dinner or as a main course for a summer luncheon.

Preheat oven to 350°F.

5   tablespoons oil
1   large onion, sliced
1   stalk celery, sliced
2   carrots, sliced
5   bay leaves
3   cloves
5   fresh or equivalent in dried sage leaves
2   teaspoons salt
3   cups dry white wine
3   pounds eye-round beef, or boned leg of veal
1   6½-ounce can tuna fish, drained
6   anchovy fillets
3   cups Mayonnaise Sauce, recipe page 69. Omit salt

Heat 3 tablespoons oil in a saucepan; add onion and cook until golden; add celery, carrots, bay leaves, cloves, sage, salt, and wine; boil for 10 minutes. Pour over meat; marinate for 24 hours in refrigerator; drain, reserving marinade. Place meat and vegetables in roasting pan with remaining 2 tablespoons of oil. Cover and roast one hour, basting occasionally with marinade. Remove from oven and cool. Cut meat into thin slices, and arrange on a serving platter. In electric blender container blend tuna and anchovy fillets until smooth; add mayonnaise sauce slowly. Pour sauce over meat and refrigerate for at least 24 hours before serving. If desired, garnish with hard-cooked egg wedges, capers, gherkins, and lemon wedges. Serves 12.

BEEF STEW WITH POTATOES
Fricandó con patate

Fricandó is the Piemontese name for *spezzatino* or stew.

- ¼ cup oil
- 2½ pounds stewing beef, cut into 1½-inch cubes
- 3 carrots, cut into 1-inch pieces
- 2 large onions, sliced thin
- 1 clove garlic, minced
- ½ teaspoon salt
- ¼ teaspoon black pepper
- 1 8-ounce can plum tomatoes, with juice
- 1 cup water
- 1 cup homemade or canned beef broth
- ½ cup dry red or white wine
- 6 medium-size potatoes, cut into 1-inch cubes

In a large skillet heat oil; brown meat on both sides; remove meat from skillet and set aside. In remaining fat, sauté carrots, onions, and garlic for 10 minutes. Return meat to skillet; add salt, pepper, tomatoes, water, broth, and wine. Cover and cook over low heat for 2 hours. Add potatoes and salt and pepper to taste; cook for 30 minutes longer. Transfer to a warm serving bowl and serve hot. Serves 6 to 8.

FINANZIERA MAMMA GIOVANNA
Finanziera Mamma Giovanna

There is no translation for this name. This recipe is my mother's version of a well-known dish of Torino; like most of her creations it is superbly delicious. It is a very elegant combination and should be used as the main course of an elegant dinner or luncheon.

2 ounces dried wild mushrooms
2 pounds of mixed chicken combs, livers, and hearts
½ pound calves' sweetbreads
2 cups homemade or canned chicken broth
6 tablespoons butter
1 pound eye-round beef, cut ¼-inch thick, then into 2-inch squares
½ cup flour
1 cup dry Marsala wine
½ teaspoon salt
¼ teaspoon white pepper
1½ tablespoons lemon juice
2 tablespoons chopped fresh parsley
8 vol-au-vent, or puff-paste patty shells, 4-inches in diameter; the frozen variety is very good.

Soak mushrooms in 1 cup of warm water for 30 minutes; rinse and drain. Wash thoroughly chicken parts and sweetbreads in cold water. In a saucepan, heat chicken broth to boiling; add chicken parts, sweetbreads, and 2 tablespoons butter; and boil vigorously for 5 minutes; drain. Place beef slices between two pieces of waxed paper and pound very thin; dip each slice in flour on both sides; shake off excess. Melt remaining 4 tablespoons butter in a large skillet; brown beef slices 1 minute on each side. Add chicken parts and sliced sweetbreads, cook 5 minutes longer. Add mushrooms and wine; cover and cook for 30 minutes at very low heat. Add salt, pepper, lemon juice, and parsley and mix well. Spoon into baked vol-au-vent. Serves 8.

MIXED BOILED MEATS
Bollito misto

This classic Torinese dish makes a beautiful party platter. Serve it with the traditional sauces.

Green Sauce, page 68
Red Sauce, page 68
Bee's Sauce, page 69

When you boil meat or poultry the excellent broth which accrues should be saved for soups and other recipes that call for chicken or beef broth. If you have left-over meat, dice it and use it in a main-dish salad. See page 98.

1   2- to 3-pound beef tongue
2   pounds fresh beef brisket
2   pounds bottom-round beef
2   veal knuckles
2   onions, sliced
2   carrots, sliced
3   cloves
2   cloves garlic
3   stalks celery, sliced
6   sprigs fresh parsley
2   bay leaves
2   teaspoons salt
1   teaspoon white pepper
water
1   4- to 5-pound capon or stewing chicken
1   cotechino sausage, cooked in a separate kettle; recipe page 108

In a large kettle, combine beef tongue, brisket, bottom round, and veal knuckles; cover generously with cold water; heat to boiling, lower heat and simmer for 30 minutes. Skim off surface scum. Add onions, carrots, cloves, garlic, celery, parsley, bay leaves, salt, pepper, and water to make 5 quarts. Again, heat to boiling; lower heat, cover and simmer for 1½ hours. Add capon or chicken and simmer for 2 hours longer. Leave in broth until serving time. Transfer to a hot serving platter and slice as you serve. Serve with cotechino, mashed potatoes and sautéed spinach. Serves 18 to 20.

BOILED BEEF SALAD

Insalata di lesso avanzato

2	cups cooked meat, diced
1	large sweet onion, sliced thin
½	pound fresh sun-ripened tomatoes, sliced
3	tablespoons blue cheese, crumbled
6	tablespoons oil
2	tablespoons wine vinegar
½	teaspoon salt
¼	teaspoon white pepper

In a salad bowl, combine meat, onions, tomatoes, blue cheese, oil, vinegar, salt, and pepper; toss gently; cover and refrigerate for 1 hour before serving. Serves 4 to 6.

PAN-BROILED STEAKS

Fettine di manzo in padella

4	slices beef eye round, ½-inch thick
½	teaspoon salt
¼	teaspoon white pepper
6	tablespoons butter
1	clove garlic, whole, but crushed lightly
¼	teaspoon rosemary leaves, crumbled
2	tablespoons brandy
½	teaspoon prepared Dijon mustard
1	tablespoon chopped fresh parsley

Season steaks with salt and pepper. Heat 2 tablespoons butter in a large skillet; add steaks; cook quickly, over high heat, on both sides until cooked as desired, rare, medium, or well done. Remove from skillet and transfer to a hot serving plate. Add remaining 4 tablespoons butter, garlic, rosemary, brandy, mustard, and parsley to skillet; simmer gently until sauce is reduced to one-half; remove garlic. Pour sauce over steaks and serve. Serves 4.

BEEF FILLETS WITH AVOCADO SAUCE

Filetto di bue con salsa di avocado

4 tablespoons butter
4 fillets of beef, cut 1-inch thick
½ teaspoon salt
¼ teaspoon white pepper
1 ripe avocado, mashed
1 tablespoon chopped fresh or frozen chives
2 tablespoons heavy cream
1 egg yolk, slightly beaten

Melt butter over high heat in a large skillet; brown fillets for 4 or 5 minutes on each side; carefully control heat to prevent butter from burning. Transfer to a warm serving dish; season with salt and pepper and keep warm. Remove skillet from heat. To juices in skillet, add avocado, chives, cream, and egg yolk; mix well. Over low heat, cook for 2 or 3 minutes, stirring constantly. Pour over fillets and serve immediately. Serves 4.

STUFFED FLANK STEAK, SERVED COLD

Rotolo di bue lessato, servito freddo

This makes a pleasing summer dish. Serve it with homemade Mayonnaise, page 69.

1 2½- to 3-pound flank steak
½ pound ground lean pork meat
3 slices stale white bread, soaked in water and squeezed dry, crumbled
3 slices boiled ham, diced
1 tablespoon pinoli (pine nuts)
4 tablespoons grated Parmesan cheese
2 eggs
1 teaspoon salt
¼ teaspoon nutmeg
2 cups canned beef broth
2 cups water
1 carrot, sliced
1 celery stalk, sliced

With a sharp knife, trim excess fat from steak. Score one surface, ⅛-inch deep in a diamond pattern. Pound steak to flatten. In a bowl, combine pork meat, bread, ham, pinoli, cheese, eggs, salt, and nutmeg. Spread stuffing over uncut side of steak; roll up and tie securely with string. Wrap in a piece of cheesecloth and tie again with string. In a kettle, combine broth with water, carrot, and celery; heat to boiling; add meat roll; lower heat and simmer for 2 hours. Let cool in liquids; remove cheesecloth, but not first set of string ties. Wrap in dry towel. Refrigerate for several hours before serving. Slice into 1-inch slices; arrange on a serving platter and serve with preferred sauce. Serves 6 to 8.

BEEF-LEMON PATTIES
Polpettine al limone

1 pound ground lean beef
juice of two lemons
2 slices white bread, crumbled
2 eggs
1 teaspoon salt
¼ teaspoon white pepper
½ cup flour
3 tablespoons butter

Place meat in a small bowl; pour lemon juice over; mix well; cover and refrigerate for 2 or 3 hours. Combine meat, bread, eggs, salt, and pepper. Form into 8 small patties; dip into flour to coat; pat and shake off excess. Melt butter in a large frying pan; over medium heat, brown patties on both sides. Serve hot. Serves 4.

MEAT LOAF WITH SPINACH
Polpettone con spinaci

Preheat oven to 350°F.
2 pounds ground lean beef
1 pound fresh spinach, steamed and chopped, or
1 10-ounce package frozen chopped spinach, thawed and drained
3 eggs, beaten
1½ teaspoons salt
½ teaspoon black pepper
2 tablespoons chopped fresh parsley
3 tablespoons unflavored bread crumbs

In a large bowl combine meat, spinach, eggs, salt, pepper, and parsley; mix well. Form into an 8-inch loaf. Place in a greased 8 × 4 × 3-inch baking dish; sprinkle with bread crumbs. Bake for 1 hour and 15 minutes. Serve in slices with favorite sauce. Serves 6.

SUMMERTIME MEAT LOAF WITH VEGETABLES
Polpettone estivo

Preheat oven to 350°F.

1	pound eggplants, peeled and cut into ¼-inch slices
2	teaspoons salt
2	tablespoons butter
2	pounds ground lean beef
2	large onions, chopped
2	cloves garlic, chopped
1	16-ounce can plum tomatoes with juices
2	bay leaves
3	tablespoons chopped fresh parsley
½	cup dry white or red wine
½	teaspoon black pepper
1	teaspoon sugar
2	tablespoons oil
1	pound zucchini, sliced ¼-inch thick
2	eggs, beaten
1½	cups white sauce, recipe page 65
½	cup grated Parmesan cheese

Sprinkle eggplant slices with 1 teaspoon salt, and set aside for 1 hour. Heat butter in skillet; add beef, stirring until brown; add onions and garlic; cook, stirring occasionally, for 5 minutes. Add tomatoes, bay leaves, parsley, wine, remaining 1 teaspoon salt, pepper, and sugar. Cover and simmer over low heat for 30 minutes. Remove from skillet. Add oil to skillet and fry zucchini for 5 minutes. Remove and drain on paper towels.

In a 14-inch bake-and-serve dish, arrange zucchini, eggplant, and meat in alternate layers, repeating until all ingredients are used, with a top layer of vegetables. Combine eggs with white sauce and pour over top of vegetables, sprinkle with cheese and bake for 45 minutes. Cut into squares and serve hot or cold. Serves 6 to 10.

BEEF STEAK BAKED WITH DUMPLINGS

Fettine di manzo con gnocchetti, al forno

Preheat oven to 400°F.
Dumplings:
 2 cups flour
 1 teaspoon salt
 ½ teaspoon nutmeg
 4 eggs
 ½ cup water
 2 tablespoons butter
Sauce and steak:
 4 tablespoons butter
 ½ pound fresh mushrooms, cleaned and sliced
 1 small onion, chopped
 1 tablespoon flour
 ¾ cup heavy cream
 ½ cup water
 ½ teaspoon salt
 ¼ teaspoon white pepper
 4 tablespoons butter
 6 slices fillet or shell of beef
 ½ pound Fontina cheese, slivered

Dumplings: In a large bowl mix flour, salt, and nutmeg; add eggs, one at a time, stir to mix. Dough will be stiff. Gradually add water, mixing dough into a soft batter. Hold colander over a large saucepan of rapidly boiling water. Pour batter into colander; with a wooden spoon, push batter through colander into boiling water. Boil dumplings for 3 minutes; drain well. Transfer to a 9 × 12-inch bake-and-serve dish; add butter, toss gently to coat dumplings; set aside in a warm place.

Sauce: Heat butter in a small saucepan; add mushrooms and onion, sauté for three or four minutes until onions are tender. Remove from heat; add flour and stir; gradually add cream, water, salt and pepper. Return saucepan to medium heat; stir constantly until sauce thickens. Lower heat and simmer, uncovered, for 3 minutes. Remove from heat and set aside. Heat remaining 4 tablespoons butter in a large skillet; sauté steaks 3 minutes on each side over medium-high heat. Transfer and arrange over the dumplings; spoon sauce over. Top with cheese. Bake for 8 to 10 minutes, until cheese is melted. Serve at once. Serves 6.

MIXED FRIED MEATS
Fritto misto

Fritto misto is one of the most impressive platters you will ever hope to serve on a special occasion, to your family or friends. In Piemonte, it is often the main course of an elegant wedding dinner. It consists of a variable number, from four to twelve dishes of meats and vegetables, all fried separately. It can be prepared in advance, but it must be cooked at the last minute, and that requires help. Remember that each recipe usually serves 6 people, so prepare only as many recipes as you will need for the number of guests you will be serving.

For a giant Fritto Misto you can use:

Breaded Scaloppine alla Piemontese, page 90
Butter-Fried Sweetbreads, page 114
Butter-Fried Calves' Brains, page 115
Butter-Fried Calves' Liver, page 115
Turkey Croquettes, page 139
Breaded Fried Mushrooms, page 164
Breaded Chicken Breasts, page 132
Butter-Fried Lamb Chops, page 111
Fried Snails, page 79
Fried Amaretti, page 192
Sweet Fried Semolino, page 194
Sautéed Asparagus, page 158
Breaded Fried Cauliflower, page 160
Fried Zucchini, page 170

LINA'S
MEAT LOAF
Polpettone alla Lina

Preheat oven to 350°F.

2 pounds lean ground beef
½ pound lean boiled ham, ground
2 eggs
½ cup grated Parmesan cheese
¼ teaspoon nutmeg
1 teaspoon salt
¼ teaspoon black pepper
½ cup flour
1 whole clove garlic
2 tablespoons butter
4 tablespoons oil
½ teaspoon dried rosemary leaves, crumbled
2 bay leaves
1 carrot
1 stalk celery
1 small onion
6 sprigs fresh parsley
2 beef bouillon cubes
½ cup hot water

In a large bowl, combine meat, ham, eggs, cheese, nutmeg, salt, and pepper; mix well and shape into a roll 4 inches in diameter. Dredge in flour and place in a baking pan with garlic, butter, oil, rosemary, and bay leaves; over medium heat, brown roll on all sides. Finely chop carrot, celery, onion and parsley; put in pan with meat roll. Dissolve bouillon cubes in hot water and add to pan. Bake for 1 hour and 30 minutes, basting occasionally with pan juices. Serves 6.

PORK SPARERIBS BAKED WITH CABBAGE
Costine di maiale al forno, con cavoli

Preheat oven to 250°F.

6 pounds spareribs, cut into serving pieces
2 beef bouillon cubes
½ cup hot water
2 cloves garlic, crushed
2 teaspoons salt
1 teaspoon white pepper
3 bay leaves
3 medium onions, sliced
1 Savoy cabbage, sliced thin

Place spareribs in a large shallow baking pan; cover with aluminum foil and bake for 1½ hours. Transfer spareribs to a large bake-and-serve dish; combine bouillon cubes dissolved in hot water, garlic, salt, pepper, bay leaves, and onions; pour over ribs. Arrange cabbage over and around ribs. Cover, return to oven; raise heat to 325°F. and bake for 35 or 40 minutes. Remove foil and bake 15 minutes longer. Serves 6.

PORK ROAST WITH BEER
Arrosto di maiale alla birra

3 tablespoons butter
1 pound onions, sliced thin
3 pounds center-cut pork loin
1 teaspoon salt
½ teaspoon white pepper
1 clove garlic, crushed
3 bay leaves
2 cups beer
1 tablespoon flour

Melt butter in a Dutch oven; add onions and cook over low heat until onions are soft and yellow. Add pork and brown on all sides. Sprinkle with salt and pepper; add garlic, bay leaves, and beer. Cover and simmer for 2½ hours. Slice and transfer to a warm platter and keep warm. Skim fat and remove bay leaves from Dutch oven. Add flour to onions and pan juices; stir and cook until thickened. Pour over meat and serve. Serves 6 to 8.

FRESH HAM WITH PORT WINE

Prosciutto fresco al Porto

3 to 4 pounds fresh pork shoulder
1½ cups port wine
3 tablespoons oil
4 bay leaves
½ teaspoon dried rosemary leaves, crumbled
1 whole clove garlic
1 medium carrot
1 medium onion
1 stalk celery
2 tablespoons chopped fresh parsley
½ teaspoon salt
¼ teaspoon black pepper
1½ cups homemade or canned beef broth
1 tablespoon flour

Place ham in a bowl; pour wine over and marinate for 2 to 4 hours, turning occasionally; pat ham dry. Reserve marinade. Heat oil with bay leaves, rosemary and garlic in a Dutch oven; add ham and brown well on all sides. Chop carrot, onion, celery and add to ham with parsley; sprinkle with salt and pepper. Add wine from marinade and cook over medium-high heat until evaporated. Add 1 cup broth; cover and simmer for 3 hours, turning ham occasionally. Transfer to a warm serving platter and keep warm. Remove fat, garlic, and bay leaves from Dutch oven. Blend flour into remaining pan juices, add remaining ½ cup broth; stir and cook until thickened. Serve sauce in a separate bowl. Serves 6 to 8.

PORK CHOPS
WITH HERBS
Costolette di maiale
aromatiche

2	tablespoons butter
1	tablespoon oil
6	pork chops, cut 1-inch thick
1/2	teaspoon salt
1/4	teaspoon black pepper
1	large onion, sliced
1/2	teaspoon dried rosemary leaves, crumbled
1/2	teaspoon dried sage leaves, crumbled
3	bay leaves
1/2	cup dry white or red wine
2	tablespoons lemon juice

In a large skillet, over medium heat, melt butter, add oil; brown pork chops on both sides. Sprinkle with salt and pepper; add onion, rosemary, sage, bay leaves, wine, and lemon juice. Cover and cook over low heat for 30 minutes. Transfer chops to a warm serving dish; pour off fat from skillet; remove bay leaves; spoon onion over chops and serve. Serves 4 to 6.

PORK STEW
WITH POTATOES
Fricandó di maiale
con patate

2	pounds boneless lean pork loin, cut into 1-inch cubes
1/2	cup flour
1	teaspoon salt
1/4	teaspoon black pepper
3	tablespoons oil
3	tablespoons tomato paste
1	cup hot water
4	bay leaves
1/4	cup vinegar
1	large onion, chopped
4	large potatoes, peeled and coarsely diced

Trim off fat from meat; rub meat with a mixture of flour, salt, and pepper. Heat oil in a Dutch oven; add meat and brown on all sides. Stir in tomato paste mixed with water, bay leaves, vinegar, and onion. Cover and cook over low heat for 1½ hours, stirring occasionally. Add potatoes, cover and cook 30 minutes longer until potatoes are tender. Check seasonings. Remove bay leaves. Transfer to a warm serving bowl and serve. Serves 6.

BOILED ITALIAN SAUSAGE
Cotechino

Cotechino is a large Italian sausage. The name is derived from *cotenna,* meaning "pork rind," which is mixed with the sausage meat. Look for it in Italian meat markets.

1   cotechino, about 1½ to 2 pounds

In a small kettle, cover sausage with water and soak for 1 hour. Prick cotechino with a fork; add more water to the kettle and bring to a boil. Lower heat; cover and simmer for 3 hours. Turn off heat and leave cotechino in hot cooking water until you are ready to serve. Transfer to a warm serving dish; cut into 1-inch slices. Serve with mashed potatoes and spinach. Serves 6.

LAMB
Agnello

ROAST LAMB WITH MUSTARD
Arrosto di agnello, alla senape

Preheat oven to 350°F.
4   tablespoons butter
8- to 10-chop rack of lamb
½   teaspoon salt
½   teaspoon white pepper
3   tablespoons Dijon mustard
1   cup unflavored bread crumbs
2   cloves garlic, finely chopped
2   tablespoon finely chopped fresh parsley

Melt butter in a roasting pan; put in lamb; sprinkle with salt and pepper; cover and roast for 1 hour, basting frequently with pan juice. Remove from oven; spread mustard over top and sides of meat. Combine bread crumbs, garlic, and parsley; carefully press onto surface of lamb. Cover and return to oven for 45 to 60 minutes, until meat is tender. Remove from oven; cut meat into chops; transfer to a warm serving dish. Serves 4 or 5.

LAMB, ALLA VALDOSTANA
Agnello alla Valdostana

6 or 7 sprigs parsley
1 large onion
1 large carrot
1 celery stalk
1 clove garlic, crushed
3-pound leg of lamb, cut into 1-inch pieces
1 teaspoon dried thyme leaves, crumbled
6 juniper berries, crushed
5 bay leaves
5 cloves
1 1-inch piece cinnamon stick
1 teaspoon salt
½ teaspoon black pepper
2 cups dry red wine
3 tablespoons oil
2 tablespoons Grappa, or brandy
1 16-ounce can plum tomatoes, drained and chopped
3 tablespoons flour
½ cup heavy cream

Combine and finely chop parsley, onion, carrot, celery, and garlic. Place lamb in a large bowl; sprinkle with chopped vegetables; add thyme, juniper berries, bay leaves, cloves, cinnamon stick, salt, and pepper. Pour wine over; cover bowl tightly and marinate in refrigerator for 3 days, turning each day. Drain lamb, using a slotted spoon; save marinade and vegetables. Heat oil in a Dutch oven; brown lamb over high heat, stirring, for 4 to 5 minutes; add brandy and cook until it has evaporated. When lamb is golden, pour marinade and vegetables over it; add tomatoes; lower heat; cover and simmer for 2 hours. Transfer lamb and vegetables to a warm deep serving dish, leaving juices in Dutch oven. Add flour to cream and mix well; stir into juices in Dutch oven; stir and cook for 5 minutes over medium heat. Pour over lamb and serve hot. Serve with polenta, recipe page 58. Serves 6 to 8.

MARINATED ROASTED LAMB
Agnello arrosto

The tender young lamb of Italy is not available in the United States. Here, we have older lamb with stronger flavor and more mature meat. Through experimenting, I have learned that by marinating lamb, as the Piemontese tenderize venison, the cooked meat becomes deliciously tender and fragrant.

Preheat oven to 425°F.

1	leg of lamb, about 6 pounds
4	cloves garlic, cut in slivers
2½	teaspoons salt
1	teaspoon black pepper
3	cups dry white wine
¼	cup oil
4	teaspoons lemon juice
1½	teaspoons grated lemon rind
½	teaspoon dried tarragon leaves, crumbled
1½	teaspoons dried rosemary leaves, crumbled
4	bay leaves

Make several cuts in meat and insert half of the slivered garlic; rub meat with a mixture of salt and pepper. Place lamb in a large bowl. Mix together wine, oil, lemon juice, lemon rind, tarragon, rosemary, and bay leaves; pour the mixture over lamb; marinate, covered, in the refrigerator overnight; turning the meat occasionally to marinate evenly. Remove lamb from marinade; reserve marinade. Place lamb in roasting pan. Roast covered for 15 minutes. Pour off fat; pour over half of reserved marinade and remaining garlic. Reduce oven heat to 325°F. and roast for 1½ hours until tender; baste several times with remaining marinade. Transfer to a warm serving platter, slice, and serve. Serves 6 to 8.

LAMB CHOP CASEROLE

Costolette d'agnello al forno

Preheat oven to 350°F.

- 6 tablespoons butter
- 12 single-rib lamb chops
- ½ teaspoon salt
- 3 medium onions, sliced
- 2 cloves garlic, minced
- ½ teaspoon dried marjoram leaves, crumbled
- 3 medium potatoes, peeled and sliced ¼ inch thick
- ½ pound fresh mushrooms, sliced
- 3 cups homemade or canned chicken broth
- ½ cup dry white wine

Melt butter in a large skillet; brown chops; lightly sprinkle with salt and remove from skillet. To remaining butter, add onions, garlic, and marjoram; cook for 10 minutes over medium-low heat. Add potatoes; cover and cook for 10 minutes; add mushrooms and cook, uncovered, for 10 minutes longer. Arrange in bottom of a bake-and-serve dish, one layer of potato mixture, then a layer of chops; alternate in layers, ending with potato mixture. Pour broth and wine over and bake, uncovered, for 40 minutes or until the chops are tender. Serves 6.

BUTTER-FRIED LAMB CHOPS

Costolette d'agnello al burro

- 3 pounds lean loin single lamb chops, cut ½-inch thick
- ¾ cup flour
- 3 eggs, well beaten
- 1¼ cup unflavored breadcrumbs
- 8 tablespoons butter
- ½ teaspoon salt
- ¼ teaspoon white pepper
- 1 lemon, cut into wedges

Pound chops thin between two pieces of waxed paper; dip into flour; shake off excess; dip into eggs, then into breadcrumbs; shake off excess. Refrigerate for 1 hour. Melt butter in a large skillet and fry chops at medium-high heat 4 minutes on each side, until golden. Transfer to a warm serving dish; sprinkle with salt and pepper and serve hot, with lemon wedges. Serves 6.

LAMB CHOPS WITH HERBS

Costolette d'agnello alla "Valle di Lanzo"

6 juniper berries
3 cloves
4 sage leaves
½ teaspoon dried rosemary leaves, crumbled
½ teaspoon thyme
1 clove garlic, crushed
1 small onion, finely chopped
½ cup dry white wine
12 single-rib lamb chops
½ teaspoon salt
¼ teaspoon black pepper
½ cup flour
2 eggs, well beaten
1 cup unflavored bread crumbs
6 tablespoons butter
3 tablespoons oil
juice of one lemon
2 tablespoons fresh parsley, chopped

Crush juniper berries and cloves; combine with sage, rosemary, thyme, garlic, onion, and wine. Pound chops as thin as possible; arrange them in a large shallow dish, and pour over herb-wine mixture; add salt and pepper; turn to coat chops with mixture. Cover and refrigerate for one hour. Drain and pat dry with paper towels. Dip each chop, on both sides, lightly, in flour, then in eggs and bread crumbs. Shake off excess crumbs. Heat butter and oil in a large skillet, and fry chops, a few at a time, for 3 to 4 minutes on each side. Transfer to a warm serving platter. To juices remaining in skillet, add lemon juice and parsley; cook for 5 minutes, stirring; pour over chops and serve at once. Serves 6.

LAMB STEW WITH MUSHROOMS
Fricandó d'agnello, con funghi

3 tablespoons butter
3 tablespoons oil
3 pounds trimmed boneless lean lamb, cut into 1-inch cubes
1 whole clove garlic
3 bay leaves
1½ teaspoon salt
½ teaspoon black pepper
1 cup water
½ cup dry white wine
1 pound fresh mushrooms, sliced

Heat butter and oil in a Dutch oven; brown lamb cubes on all sides. Add garlic, bay leaves, salt, pepper, water, and wine. Cover and cook over low heat for 2 hours. Remove garlic and bay leaves; add mushrooms and cook, uncovered, for 15 minutes longer. Transfer to a warm serving dish. Serve with boiled rice. Serves 6.

LAMB STEW WITH ONIONS AND PEAS
Spezzatino d'agnello, con cipolline e piselli

Preheat oven to 350°F.

2 tablespoons butter
2 tablespoons oil
2 pounds trimmed boneless lamb, cut into 1-inch cubes
2 small onions, quartered
1 clove garlic, chopped
2 tablespoons flour
1 teaspoon salt
½ teaspoon black pepper
1 cup homemade or canned beef broth
4 canned plum tomatoes, chopped
½ teaspoon dried thyme, crumbled
1 celery stalk with leaves and 2 sprigs of parsley, tied together
1 pound small white onions, peeled
2 pounds fresh unshelled peas, or 1 10-ounce package frozen peas
2 tablespoons chopped fresh parsley

In a large skillet melt butter; add oil; brown lamb cubes on all sides. Add quartered onions, garlic, and flour; cook, stirring for 5 minutes. Add salt, pepper, broth, tomatoes, thyme, and celery with parsley. Stir and transfer to a large casserole or baking pan; cover tightly; cook in oven for 1 hour. Remove celery with parsley; add small onions and peas; cover and return to oven and cook 20 minutes longer. Sprinkle with chopped parsley before serving. Serves 6.

LAMB STEW LANZO VALLEY
Agnello in umido, della Valle di Lanzo

4	tablespoons butter
2	whole cloves garlic
½	teaspoon dried rosemary leaves, crumbled
2	bay leaves
2	pounds lean lamb shoulder, cut into 1-inch cubes
1	16-ounce can plum tomatoes
½	cup dry vermouth
2	beef bouillon cubes

Melt butter in a large skillet; add garlic, rosemary, bay leaves, and cook over low heat for 5 minutes. Add lamb cubes; over high heat brown cubes on all sides. Add tomatoes and juice, vermouth and bouillon cubes; cover, reduce heat to low and simmer for 2 hours. Stir occasionally and, if necessary, add a little hot water. Remove garlic and bay leaves. Transfer stew to a warm deep serving dish. Serve with noodles. Serves 4 to 6.

VARIETY MEATS
Frattaglie

BUTTER-FRIED SWEETBREADS
Animelle al burro

3	pairs calves' sweetbreads
1	teaspoon salt
½	cup flour
8	tablespoons butter

Soak sweetbreads in cold water for 30 minutes; drain. In saucepan, cover sweetbreads with water; add ½ teaspoon salt; heat to boiling; lower heat and simmer for 10 minutes. Drain and immediately rinse under running cold water for two minutes. Remove tissue and cartilage; place sweetbreads between 2 pieces of waxed paper and flatten with a weight. Cut into slices ½-inch thick; dip slices into flour to coat; shake off excess. Heat butter in a large skillet over medium heat and cook sweetbreads on both sides until golden. Transfer to a warm serving dish; sprinkle with remaining ½ teaspoon salt. Pour over butter from pan. Serve hot. Serves 6.

BUTTER-FRIED CALVES' BRAINS
Cervella al burro

2	calves' brains
¾	cup flour
2	eggs, beaten
1½	cups unflavored breadcrumbs
8	tablespoons butter
½	teaspoon salt
1	lemon, cut into wedges

Soak brains in cold water for 15 minutes; remove membranes and veins; rinse and drain; cut into serving pieces. Dip each piece into flour; flatten with your hand, then dip into beaten eggs, then into breadcrumbs; shake off excess. Melt butter in frying pan; cook brains, a few pieces at a time, until golden on both sides; transfer to a warm serving dish; sprinkle with salt. Pour butter from pan over brains; serve hot with lemon wedges. Serves 4 to 6.

BUTTER-FRIED CALVES' LIVER
Fegato di vitello, al burro

2	pounds calves' liver, thinly sliced
¾	cup flour
8	tablespoons butter
½	teaspoon salt
1	lemon, cut into wedges

Dip liver into flour; shake off excess. Melt butter in a large skillet and fry liver for 1 minute on each side. Transfer to a warm serving dish; sprinkle with salt and serve at once with lemon wedges. Serves 6.

FRESH BEEF TONGUE IN GREEN SAUCE
Lingua di bue in salsa verde

1 3- to 4-pound fresh beef tongue
1 tablespoon salt
2 small onions
3 bay leaves
1 cup vinegar, reserve 3 tablespoons for sauce
6 tablespoons butter
4 tablespoons flour
2 cups homemade or canned beef broth, heated
½ teaspoon salt
¼ teaspoon white pepper
½ cup chopped fresh parsley
2 cloves garlic, minced

Wash tongue and place in a large kettle; add salt, onions, bay leaves, and vinegar; cover with cold water. Bring to a boil; lower heat; cover tightly and simmer for 3 hours. Allow tongue to cool in broth. Remove all skin, fat, and bones; cut into ¼-inch slices; set aside. Strain broth, then keep hot.

Melt 4 tablespoons butter in a small saucepan over low heat; add flour, stir continuously for 2 minutes without browning flour. Add hot broth all at once. Sauce will thicken automatically as it comes to a boil. Season with salt and pepper. In a large skillet melt remaining 2 tablespoons butter and sauté parsley and garlic for 2 or 3 minutes; add 3 tablespoons of reserved vinegar; simmer for 4 minutes; blend into thickened sauce; add sliced tongue; cover and simmer over low heat for 10 minutes. Serves 8 to 10.

KIDNEYS WITH MARSALA WINE
Rognone al Marsala

Marsala, a product of Sicily, is a fortified sweet wine with a sherry-like flavor and color; it is used in cooking, and, of course, for drinking, in all parts of Italy. There are gradations of sweetness in the various vintages, classified from *secco* (dry) to *dolce* (very sweet).

4 veal kidneys
½ cup vinegar
4 tablespoons butter
1 medium onion, sliced
½ cup dry Marsala wine
½ teaspoon salt
¼ teaspoon white pepper

Slice kidneys ¼-inch thick. Place in a small bowl; pour vinegar over and let stand for 1 hour. Drain and pat dry with paper towels. Melt butter in a skillet; cook onion until golden; add kidney and cook over medium-high heat for 3 or 4 minutes, stirring occasionally. Add wine; increase heat and cook until wine is reduced in half. Add salt and pepper. Transfer to a warm serving dish and serve hot. Serves 6.

CALVES' LIVER ASTI-STYLE
Fegato all'Astigiana

3 onions
2 cloves garlic, minced
6 sprigs fresh parsley
4 slices of bacon
4 tablespoons butter
2 pounds calves' liver, thinly sliced
1 tablespoon flour
½ cup Barbera (red) wine
½ teaspoon salt
½ teaspoon white pepper

In wooden bowl, combine onions, garlic, parsley, and bacon; chop very fine. Melt butter in a skillet; add onion mixture and cook over medium-high heat until onions turn golden. Add liver and cook for 1 minute on each side. Sprinkle with flour; add wine; cover and cook, over low heat, for 15 minutes. Sprinkle with salt and pepper; transfer to a warm serving dish and serve at once. Serves 6.

7

Poultry and Game

Pollame e Selvaggina

Chicken comes to the Piemontese table in splendid guises. For a festive dinner, you might be served a chicken roll in brandied aspic, or a delicate young hen, braised with small white onions and smothered in wine sauce. On a summer evening, a likely favorite would be a boned bird, chilled under a blanket of tuna sauce. In every kitchen, chicken is cooked with fragrant herbs to enhance the flavor.

It was in the Piemonte town of Marengo that "Pollo alla Marengo" was created for the Little Emperor. Here you find the true story of Napoleon's legendary dish, and the true recipe, as well.

In the late fall, when the hunting season is open in Piemonte, the large selection of game offers endless adventures in good eating. If you do not have a hunter in your family, and game birds are not available, fresh or frozen, use the humble chicken in a recipe that calls for pheasant, or Cornish hen, and you will be pleasantly surprised.

PAN-ROASTED CHICKEN NONNO ANTONIO

Gallet al babi, Pollo in padella, Nonno Antonio

I must translate the Piemontese name for this recipe. *Gallet* means young rooster. *Babi* means toad; the relationship of the two is that you have to flatten the chicken so that it resembles a squatting toad. This recipe brings to mind pleasant memories of my youth. I wish you could have known my grandfather, Antonio. He was the grandfather that I wish everybody could have had: loving, cheerful, and most of all, a wonderful person. Any excuse was good for a picnic, as far as Nonno Antonio was concerned. All he needed were some children and one or two "gallet al babi" and away we went, by foot, by bicycle, or by horsedrawn carriage, sometimes by rowboat or even by funicular railway, on our way to a new adventure.

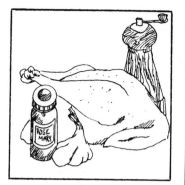

1 2- to 2½-pound broiling chicken
4 tablespoons butter
6 tablespoons oil
1 teaspoon salt
½ teaspoon white pepper
1 teaspoon dried rosemary leaves
2 whole cloves garlic

Wash and dry chicken; split open along back bone; crack breast-bone and spread chicken as flat as possible. Rub with butter, salt, and pepper. Heat oil in a heavy skillet with the rosemary and garlic; cook over low heat for 5 minutes; discard rosemary and garlic. Arrange chicken in oil, breast side down; on top of chicken place a cover with a weight on top to keep the chicken flat. Cook over medium high heat for 10 minutes; turn chicken and cook for 10 minutes longer; again, turn it over for another 10 minutes. Now, it should be ready to serve. It is delicious hot, but also very good cold, so pack it up for your next picnic. I have tried this recipe in my oven broiler but it does not taste the same as when cooked in the skillet. Serves 4.

CHICKEN BAKED IN SALT
Pollo arrostito al sale

You will have to try this recipe to believe its goodness! For this recipe please do not use a thawed frozen chicken, use the best chicken you can find and you will have a wonderful feast. The only salt you will have to discard is the salt from the bottom of the pan, because it will have absorbed all the fat. Keep the remaining salt for another time.

Preheat oven to 400°F.
1 5-pound roasting chicken
6 pounds coarse kosher salt

Wash chicken and pat dry with paper towel. Place 2 inches of salt in a deep roasting pan. Truss legs and wings of chicken to preserve the shape. Place over salt in pan. Pour remaining salt over chicken; shake pan so that salt will fill all spaces and cover chicken. If the pan is not high enough, make a collar around the edge of heavy aluminum foil tied firmly with string. Bake for 2 hours. Remove from oven. The salt will have hardened, so break it off with a hammer. Using a kitchen brush, remove salt from chicken and serve. Serves 6.

BAKED CHICKEN WITH HERBS "BELVEDERE"
Pollo aromatico, "Belvedere"

Preheat oven to 425°F.
 1 3-pound roasting chicken
 3 tablespoons butter, softened
 2 teaspoons dried rosemary leaves, crumbled
 2 teaspoons dried marjoram leaves, crumbled
 1 clove garlic, minced
 1 teaspoon salt
 ½ teaspoon black pepper
 3 tablespoons oil

Sauce:
 3 tablespoons butter
 1 small onion, chopped
 ½ teaspoon dried rosemary leaves, crumbled
 ½ teaspoon dried marjoram leaves, crumbled
 1 whole clove garlic
 2 tablespoons flour
 1 cup dry white wine
 ½ cup light cream
 ½ cup homemade or canned chicken broth

Wash chicken and pat dry. Mix together 1 tablespoon butter, one teaspoon rosemary, one teaspoon marjoram, half each of garlic, salt, and pepper; rub inside of chicken with mixture; secure opening with string. Use remaining butter to rub outside of chicken; sprinkle with remaining herbs, garlic, salt and pepper. Place chicken, breast side up, in a roasting pan and bake at 450°F. uncovered, for 30 minutes. Pour oil over chicken; reduce oven temperature to 350°F. and cook for 30 minutes longer. Meanwhile, make sauce: in a small saucepan melt butter; add onion and sauté until light golden in color; add rosemary, marjoram and clove of garlic; cook until garlic turns brown. Remove saucepan from heat; discard garlic; stir in flour and gradually add wine, cream, broth and, if necessary, salt and pepper to taste. Return to heat; bring to a boil; lower heat and cook gently for 5 minutes. Transfer chicken to a warm serving platter; serve sauce in a separate bowl. Serves 4 to 6.

CHICKEN ALLA MARENGO, ALESSANDRIA

Pollo alla Marengo, Alessandria

After one of his great victories in 1800, Napoleon and his staff walked into the only inn they could find in Marengo, a very small town in the province of Alessandria, to ask for some food. The woman, who was the owner and cook, put together all the edible ingredients she had. The dish turned out to be so good that it is still famous today in numerous versions.

1   3-pound frying chicken, cut in pieces
½   cup flour
6   tablespoons butter
3   tablespoons oil
1   16-ounce can plum tomatoes with juice
½   pound fresh mushrooms, sliced
2   tablespoons chopped fresh parsley
2   whole cloves garlic
1   teaspoon salt
½   teaspoon black pepper
2   cups dry white wine
juice of one lemon
6   eggs
6   large shrimps (in the original recipe crayfish were used)
6   slices of white toasting bread

Wash chicken pieces and pat dry with paper towels; dredge in flour and shake off excess. In large skillet, melt 4 tablespoons of butter; add oil and brown the chicken on all sides. Add tomatoes and juice, mushrooms, parsley, garlic, salt, and pepper. Cover and cook over low heat. Add wine and lemon juice; cook, uncovered, for 30 minutes longer, discard garlic. In a separate frying pan, melt remaining butter; fry eggs and shrimps. Remove crust from bread and fry each slice until golden on both sides. Transfer chicken pieces to a warm serving platter; pour sauce over; arrange slices of bread around edge of platter and top each slice with one fried egg and one shrimp. Serves 6.

CHICKEN CACCIATORA "BELVEDERE"

Pollo alla cacciatora "Belvedere"

It seems that we owe the success of this world-famous dish to a tired hunter who came home, after many hours of search for wild mushrooms, with only a few of the beautiful "porcini," and told his wife to just throw them in with the already-cooking chicken, because there were not enough for anything else. It turned out to be a delicious combination. Try it with the dried imported mushrooms available here and you will be as delighted as they were.

2	ounces dried wild mushrooms
1	4- to 5-pound roasting chicken, cut in pieces
½	cup flour
1	teaspoon salt
¼	teaspoon black pepper
6	tablespoons butter
¾	cup thinly sliced onions
½	teaspoon rosemary leaves, crumbled
1	whole clove garlic
¾	cup dry white wine or dry vermouth
2	tablespoons tomato paste

Soak mushrooms in 1 cup of lukewarm water for 15 minutes; rinse, drain and chop coarsely; set aside. Wash chicken pieces and pat dry. Mix flour, salt, and pepper; dredge chicken pieces in mixture; shake off excess. Melt butter in a large skillet; add onions, rosemary, and garlic; cook at medium heat until onions are golden. Add chicken pieces and brown gently on all sides, turning them several times. Discard garlic. Stir in wine, tomato paste, and mushrooms. Cover and cook over low heat for 1 hour. Before serving, taste and add salt and pepper, if needed. Transfer to a warm serving dish and serve. Serves 4 to 6.

CHICKEN WITH CREAM SAUCE "BELVEDERE"
Pollo alla panna, "Belvedere"

1   3- to 4-pound frying chicken, cut in pieces
4   tablespoons butter
½   teaspoon rosemary leaves, crumbled
½   teaspoon salt
¼   teaspoon white pepper
¼   teaspoon nutmeg
1   cup heavy cream

Wash chicken pieces and pat dry. Melt butter in a large skillet; add rosemary; add chicken pieces and brown slowly on all sides. Add salt, pepper, nutmeg, and cream. Cover and cook slowly for 30 minutes. Transfer into a warm serving platter; pour sauce over and serve hot. Serves 6.

CHICKEN WITH LEMON SAUCE ALLA PETER
Pollo al limone, alla Peter

This dish is named after my son because, after Vitello Tonnato, this is his favorite dish.

1   3-pound frying chicken, cut in pieces
4   tablespoons butter
4   tablespoons oil
2   bay leaves
2   medium onions, sliced
1   tablespoon flour
¾   cup dry white wine
¾   cup homemade or canned chicken broth, heated
1   teaspoon sugar
½   teaspoon salt
¼   teaspoon white pepper
3   whole lemons, sliced ¼-inch thick

Wash and dry chicken pieces. In a large skillet melt butter; stir in oil, bay leaves, and onions. Brown chicken pieces on all sides; sprinkle with flour; stir and cook for 10 minutes. Add wine and boil briskly for 2 or 3 minutes to reduce wine to half; add hot broth, sugar, salt, pepper, and lemon slices. Cover and cook over low heat until chicken is tender, about 45 to 60 minutes. Remove and discard bay leaves and lemon slices; transfer chicken to a warm serving dish. Place skillet over high heat and boil briskly for 2 to 3 minutes, to thicken remaining sauce. Pour over chicken and serve. Serves 4 to 6.

CHICKEN STEW PEASANT-STYLE

Pollo in umido alla paesana

1 4-pound stewing chicken, cut in pieces
4 slices bacon, chopped
3 tablespoons butter
3 tablespoons oil
2 medium onions, sliced thin
1 stalk celery, chopped
1 cup dry white wine
1 teaspoon salt
½ teaspoon black pepper
1 tablespoon tomato paste
2 bay leaves
2 cloves
4 medium-size potatoes, peeled and diced
2 carrots, cut into ¼-inch slices

Wash chicken and dry with paper towels. Brown bacon in a large skillet; pour off fat. Heat butter in skillet, add oil and brown chicken on all sides. Add onions and celery; cover and cook over low heat for 15 minutes. Add wine, salt, pepper, tomato paste diluted in ½ cup of warm water, bay leaves, and cloves; cover and cook over low heat for 1 hour. Add potatoes and carrots; cook 15 to 20 minutes, until chicken and vegetables are tender. During cooking, turn chicken pieces occasionally and, if necessary, add 2 or 3 tablespoons of warm water, to prevent drying. Remove bay leaves and cloves. Transfer to a warm serving bowl and serve. Serves 6 to 8.

BAKED CHICKEN SIGNOR ANTONIO
Pollo al forno Signor Antonio

Preheat oven to 400°F.

- 1 2½-pound frying chicken, cut in pieces
- ½ cup flour
- 1 teaspoon salt
- ½ teaspoon black pepper
- 2 tablespoons chopped fresh parsley
- 1 tablespoon chopped fresh tarragon leaves

grated rind of one lemon

- 1 egg
- 1 cup milk
- 4 tablespoons butter
- ¼ cup oil
- 2 teaspoons dried rosemary leaves, crumbled
- 4 slices white bread, cut into 4 triangles each, crusts removed

Wash chicken pieces and pat dry with paper towels. Combine flour, salt, pepper, parsley, tarragon, and lemon rind. Beat egg and milk together. Dip chicken pieces in egg-milk mixture, then dredge in flour-herb mixture. Chill for one hour in refrigerator. Melt 2 tablespoons of butter in a large shallow baking dish; add oil, rosemary, and chicken; turn pieces to coat them with butter and oil. Bake for 45 to 50 minutes. Sauté bread triangles in remaining 2 tablespoons butter; transfer chicken to a warm serving platter; arrange bread triangles around it. Serves 4 to 6.

BAKED CHICKEN WITH PEACHES
Pollo con pesche d'Asti, al forno

The best substitute that I have found for Asti's peaches are the canned, freestone variety from the West Coast.

Preheat oven to 375°F.

- 1½ pounds chicken thighs
- 1½ pounds chicken legs
- 1 teaspoon salt
- 4 tablespoons butter
- 4 tablespoons oil
- 1½ cups drained and mashed canned yellow peaches
- ½ teaspoon cinnamon

Wash chicken parts and pat dry with paper towels. Sprinkle with salt. Heat butter with oil in large skillet; brown chicken pieces a few pieces at a time, quickly on all sides; transfer to a large shallow bake-and-serve dish. Spoon peaches over; sprinkle with cinnamon. Cover and bake for 35 minutes; remove cover for last 10 minutes. Serve hot. Serves 6.

CHICKEN CASSEROLE WITH VERMOUTH
Pollo al forno, con vermouth

This chicken casserole would make an ideal dish for your next party. It has exotic flavor, can be prepared in advance, and is easy to serve.

Preheat oven to 350°F.

    2 ounces dried wild mushrooms
    3 pounds chicken legs
    3 pounds chicken thighs
    6 or more tablespoons butter
  ½ cup chopped onions
    1 clove garlic, chopped
    5 tablespoons flour
  ½ teaspoon white pepper
    3 chicken-bouillon cubes, crushed
    2 cups homemade or canned chicken broth
    2 teaspoons dried tarragon leaves, crumbled
 1½ cups dry vermouth

Soak dried mushrooms for 30 minutes in lukewarm water; drain and chop fine. Wash chicken pieces and dry with paper towels. In a large Dutch oven, heat 4 tablespoons butter; brown chicken pieces, a few at a time, on all sides, adding more butter as needed. In a small saucepan, over low heat, cook 2 tablespoons of butter, mushrooms, onions, and garlic for 10 minutes. Remove from heat; add flour, pepper, and bouillon cubes and stir until well blended; return to heat; gradually add chicken broth; bring to a boil and remove. Return chicken pieces to Dutch oven; sprinkle with tarragon; stir in vermouth and mushroom mixture; cover and bake for 1 hour. Transfer chicken to a warm serving platter and pour sauce over it. Serves 8 to 10.

BRAISED CHICKEN WITH SMALL WHITE ONIONS
Pollo in umido, con cipolline d'Ivrea

The sweet, small, yellow onions of Ivrea are not available in the United States but the small white ones you find in supermarkets are a good substitute.

3 tablespoons butter
3 tablespoons oil
1½ pounds small white onions, peeled
1 clove garlic, minced
1 2- to 3-pound frying chicken, cut up
2 tablespoons flour
1 cup dry white wine
1 teaspoon salt
½ teaspoon white pepper
1 teaspoon dry rosemary leaves, crumbled

In a large skillet, heat butter and oil; add onions and garlic; sauté onions until golden; transfer onions to a dish and set aside; add chicken pieces to fat in skillet. Brown on all sides, turning as needed. Remove skillet from heat; pour off all but 2 tablespoons of fat; sprinkle chicken in skillet with flour; gradually add wine, stirring; sprinkle with salt and pepper. Return onions to skillet; cover and simmer at low heat for 30 to 40 minutes, until chicken is tender. Transfer to a warm serving platter and serve. Serves 4.

CHICKEN BREASTS ALL'ASTIGIANA
Petti di pollo all'Astigiana

3 whole chicken breasts, cut in half and boned
8 tablespoons melted butter
½ cup chopped fresh parsley
1 teaspoon salt
⅛ teaspoon white pepper
6 slices thin Italian prosciutto cut in half
6 slices thin Fontina or Gruyère cheese, cut in half
4 tablespoons flour
2 teaspoons paprika
1 cup homemade or canned chicken broth
¼ cup brandy

Skin chicken breasts and cut each in half; pound each piece thin between two pieces of waxed paper; brush inside of each with butter; sprinkle with parsley, salt, and pepper. Top each piece with one slice of prosciutto and one slice of cheese. Roll up each piece and tie securely with a string. Coat chicken rolls in a mixture of flour and paprika. Heat remaining butter in a large skillet; saute chicken rolls until golden on all sides. Add chicken broth; cover and simmer for 30 minutes, basting occasionally. Remove chicken rolls from skillet and place in warm serving dish; return skillet to high heat; add brandy; stir and scrape to loosen brown bits from bottom and sides of skillet; pour sauce over chicken rolls and serve hot. Serves 6.

CHICKEN BREASTS ALLA VALDOSTANA
Petti di pollo alla Valdostana

Preheat oven to 400°F.

3	whole chicken breasts, cut in half
2	eggs, beaten
½	cup flour
4	tablespoons butter
4	tablespoons oil
½	teaspoon salt
¼	teaspoon white pepper
¾	cup diced lean boiled ham
3	tablespoons tomato paste
1	teaspoon dried marjoram leaves, crumbled
¼	cup dry Marsala wine
6	slices Fontina cheese, cut in half
½	cup homemade of canned chicken broth, heated
1	chicken-bouillon cube, crushed
1	small truffle (optional)

Remove skin and bones from chicken breasts; wash and dry with paper towels. Dip each piece in beaten eggs, then in flour. Heat butter in a large skillet; add oil; over medium heat, sauté chicken breasts for 3 minutes on each side; transfer to a large bake-and-serve dish; sprinkle with salt and pepper. In a small bowl, mix ham, tomato paste, marjoram, and wine. Arrange one piece of cheese over each piece of chicken; top with one tablespoon of ham-tomato mixture. Gently pour hot broth into bottom of baking dish (not over chicken pieces); add bouillon cube; cover with aluminum foil and bake for 15 minutes. If you decide to use the truffle, slice it very thin and sprinkle over the chicken just before serving. Serves 6.

BREADED CHICKEN BREASTS ELEGANTE
Petti di pollo panati, eleganti

4	chicken breasts, boned
1/2	cup flour
1/2	teaspoon salt
1/4	teaspoon white pepper
2	eggs, well beaten
1	cup unflavored bread crumbs
4	tablespoons butter
4	tablespoons oil

Cut chicken breasts into 2-inch × 1-inch strips. Dip strips into a mixture of flour, salt, and pepper; shake off excess; dip strips in eggs and then in bread crumbs; shake off excess. Refrigerate for 1 hour. Melt butter in a large skillet; add oil. Sauté chicken until golden brown on both sides. Transfer to a warm serving dish. Garnish with lettuce cups, containing chopped parsley, rolled anchovies, capers, sieved white and yolk of hard-cooked egg and lemon wedges. Serves 6.

CHILLED CHICKEN WITH TUNA SAUCE
Pollo freddo, in salsa tonnata

1 2- to 3-pound roasting chicken
1 large onion, quartered
2 celery stalks, cut into 2-inch pieces
2 carrots, cut into 2-inch pieces
1 whole clove garlic
3 peppercorns
2 bay leaves
3 sprigs fresh parsley
1 teaspoon salt
½ cup lemon juice
¼ teaspoon white pepper
1 6½-ounce can tuna fish in oil, reserve oil
1 tablespoon capers
4 anchovy fillets
oil to make half cup when combined with tuna oil
¼ cup chopped fresh parsley
3 hard-cooked eggs, cut in wedges
2 tablespoons red pimiento strips

Place washed chicken with onion, celery, carrots, garlic, peppercorns, bay leaves, parsley, and salt in a kettle with water to cover. Heat to boiling; lower heat and simmer for 1 hour. Cool chicken in broth. Save broth for future use. Remove skin and bones from chicken; arrange meat prices in a shallow serving dish; sprinkle with 3 tablespoons lemon juice and pepper; set aside. To make sauce, chop tuna, capers, anchovy fillets, oil, remaining 3 tablespoons lemon juice, and parsley in electric blender for 2 minutes, then blend for 1 minute, or until mixture reaches consistency of heavy cream. If more liquid is needed, add 2 tablespoons of chicken broth. Pour and spread sauce over chicken pieces; cover with plastic wrap and marinate overnight in refrigerator. Remove from refrigerator 30 minutes before serving time; garnish with hard-cooked egg wedges and pimiento strips. Serves 6.

CHICKEN ROLL IN BRANDIED ASPIC
Rotolo di pollo in gelatina

Preheat oven to 350°F.

1	3-pound chicken
1/3	cup bread crumbs
1	teaspoon salt
1/2	teaspoon white pepper
1/4	cup chopped fresh parsley
2	tablespoons chopped fresh chives
1/2	pound baked ham
1/4	pound Italian prosciutto
4	hard-cooked eggs
4	tablespoons butter
1/4	teaspoon paprika
6	strips of bacon
3	tablespoons oil
1/2	teaspoon rosemary leaves, crumbled

Bone chicken, or have the butcher do it for you; cut chicken down the back; remove wings, neck, and giblets. With the bones, make a light chicken soup, for another meal. Spread chicken, skin-side down; open like a book, and pound flat. In a small bowl combine bread crumbs, 1/2 teaspoon salt, 1/4 teaspoon pepper, parsley, and chives. Arrange ham over chicken; sprinkle with some of bread crumb mixture. Arrange prosciutto over; add more bread crumb mixture. Place whole eggs lengthwise across center of chicken. Fold in ends of chicken and, beginning at a long side, roll chicken tightly around the eggs; tie roll with string. Rub with 2 tablespoons butter; sprinkle with remaining salt, pepper, and paprika; top with bacon strips. Melt remaining tablespoon butter in baking pan; add oil and rosemary leaves; place chicken roll in oil and bake for 50 minutes, basting several times with fat from pan. Remove and discard bacon; increase heat to 425°F.; bake roll for 10 minutes longer. Cool at room temperature, and chill overnight.

For Aspic:
- 3 cups homemade or canned chicken broth
- 1 cup white wine vinegar
- 4 envelopes unflavored gelatine
- ½ teaspoon salt
- ¼ teaspoon white pepper
- 2 egg whites
- 2 egg shells, crushed
- 2 tablespoons brandy

In a saucepan, combine chicken broth, vinegar, gelatine, salt, pepper, egg whites and egg shells; heat slowly, stirring constantly until mixture comes to a boil. Remove from heat; add brandy. Strain mixture through a cloth. Cool. Pour about ½ inch aspic into a large, deep, serving platter. Place in refrigerator for 30 minutes to one hour to set. Slice chicken roll into 1-inch slices; arrange slices on top of set gelatine. Cover with remaining gelatine. Return to refrigerator overnight. Serve cold. Serves 6.

CHICKEN ASPIC
Pollo in gelatina

- 4 chicken breasts, boned and halved
- 3 cups cold water
- ½ cup white vinegar
- 1 carrot, cut into pieces
- 2 stalks celery, cut into pieces
- 1 small onion, cut in half
- 1 teaspoon salt
- ½ teaspoon white pepper

For Aspic:
- 2 envelopes unflavored gelatine
- 2 cups strained chicken broth, obtained from cooking chicken
- ¾ cup white vinegar
- 12 black olives
- 1 small jar pimiento pieces

Place chicken in a kettle; add water, vinegar, carrot, celery, onion, salt, and pepper. Heat to boiling; lower heat, cover and simmer for 30 minutes. Remove chicken from broth and cool. Add gelatine to 1 cup of cold broth to soften; place over low heat and stir until gelatine is dissolved. Remove from heat and stir in remaining broth and vinegar. Pour half of the mixture into a deep serving dish and chill in refrigerator until almost firm. Remove from refrigerator and arrange chicken breasts on top of firm gelatine; garnish with olives and pimiento strips. Cover with remaining gelatine. Chill until firm. Serves 8.

STUFFED CAPON "BELVEDERE"

Cappone ripieno "Belvedere"

Preheat oven to 350°F.

1 5-pound capon
1 cup dry white wine
2 tablespoons vinegar
1 teaspoon salt
2 cloves garlic, minced
1 teaspoon rosemary leaves, crumbled
3 small onions, cut in half
3 tablespoons butter
1 pound canned chestnuts (or ½ pound dried, soaked and strained chestnuts)
½ teaspoon white pepper
⅛ teaspoon nutmeg
3 slices white toasting bread, crusts removed, cut in small cubes
2 tablespoons flour

Wash capon and dry with paper towels. Place in a large bowl. In a small bowl, mix wine, vinegar, salt, garlic, rosemary, and onions; pour over capon and marinate for 6 hours, turning several times. In a large frying pan, sauté onions from marinade in butter for 5 minutes; add chestnuts. With potato masher, mash onion and chestnuts; stir in pepper and nutmeg; add bread cubes and stir again until well mixed. Remove capon from marinade and dry with paper towel; stuff with chestnut mixture and tie the opening together with poultry skewers or string. Place capon, breast-side up in a roasting pan, and bake uncovered for 2 to 2½ hours, until capon is tender and browned. Remove to a warm large serving platter and keep warm. Pour off all but 3 tablespoons of fat from roasting pan; blend in flour, and, stirring constantly, add 1 cup of marinade. Stir until gravy thickens. Serve gravy in a separate bowl. Serves 6 to 8.

BAKED CORNISH HENS
Gallinette Americane al forno

In Italy, Cornish hens are called "Gallinette Americane," which, translated literally, means "little American chickens."

Preheat oven to 325°F.

2	1-pound Cornish hens
1	pound onions
½	pound carrots
4	celery stalks
2	cloves garlic
4	bay leaves
4	cloves
½	teaspoon dried thyme, crumbled
½	teaspoon dried marjoram, crumbled
1	teaspoon salt
½	teaspoon black pepper
1	cup white vinegar
½	cup oil

Cut hens in half; wash and pat dry. Finely chop onions, carrots, celery, and garlic. Arrange hens in a Dutch oven; top them with chopped vegetables. Add bay leaves, cloves, thyme, marjoram, salt, and pepper; pour vinegar and oil over; cover and bake for 2 hours. Transfer hens to a warm platter; transfer vegetables and juices from the Dutch oven to electric blender; blend for 2 minutes; return to Dutch oven and thicken sauce over high heat. Pour over hens and serve hot. Serves 4.

PHEASANT OR CORNISH HENS AL CIVET

Fagiano o gallinette americane al civet

Civet is the Piemontese word for dishes of game birds, and venison, marinated and cooked in wine with chives. I believe it comes from the French word *cive*, which means "chives." Pheasant are not always available, but I have found that Cornish hens are good substitutes.

Preheat oven to 350°F.

2 3-pound pheasants or 4 1-pound Cornish hens, cut into serving pieces
2 medium onions, sliced
1 carrot, diced
1 stalk celery, diced
1 2-inch cinnamon stick
5 whole cloves
6 juniper berries
1 26-ounce bottle dry white wine
¼ pound fresh lard
1 medium onion
6 tablespoons butter
2 ounces rum
2 tablespoons flour
1 teaspoon salt
½ teaspoon white pepper
1 small truffle, thinly sliced (optional)
3 teaspoons chopped fresh or frozen chives

Thaw pheasants or Cornish hens, if frozen; wash and pat dry. In a large bowl, combine poultry pieces, half of onion slices, carrot, celery, cinnamon stick, cloves, juniper berries, and wine; stir to mix; cover and marinate in refrigerator for 24 hours. The following day, place lard and chopped onion in baking pan; add 3 tablespoons of butter and cook for several minutes, until onion turns golden; add poultry pieces and brown for 5 minutes. Add marinade of wine and vegetables, rum, flour, salt, and pepper; cover and bake 1 hour and 30 minutes. Transfer poultry pieces to heated serving platter and keep warm. Force vegetables, scrapings, and liquid from the pan through a sieve. Return sieved contents to baking pan; add remaining 3 tablespoons butter, truffle, and chives; stir over low heat for 2 or 3 minutes. Pour over pheasant or hen pieces and serve hot. This dish is traditionally served with polenta. Serves 6 to 8.

TURKEY CROQUETTES
Croqui' di tacchino

When Thanksgiving or Christmas dinners are over, everyone ends up with turkey leftovers. This recipe suggests a good way of using all the small pieces of meat.

    1   cup unflavored bread crumbs
    1   small onion, finely chopped
    2   tablespoons chopped fresh parsley
    3   eggs
 1½   teaspoons salt
   ¼   teaspoon white pepper
    3   cups coarsely chopped, cooked turkey
    6   tablespoons butter
    3   tablespoons oil

In a large bowl, combine ½ cup bread crumbs, onion, parsley, 2 eggs, salt, pepper and turkey; mix well. Shape a tablespoon of mixture into an egg-shaped croquette. Beat remaining egg; dip croquettes into egg, then into breadcrumbs; shake off excess and refrigerate for 1 hour. Melt butter in a skillet; add oil; sauté croquettes over medium-high heat until golden brown on all sides; drain on paper towels and serve hot. Serves 6.

DUCK "BELVEDERE"-STYLE

Anitra alla "Belvedere"

Preheat oven to 350°F.

- 1 4- to 5-pound duck
- 1 teaspoon salt
- ½ teaspoon white pepper
- 1 stalk celery, chopped
- 2 cloves garlic, crushed
- 4 bay leaves
- 1 cup dry Marsala wine
- 1 tablespoon capers
- 1 teaspoon Worcestershire
- 2 cups homemade or canned chicken broth, hot
- 1 small truffle (optional)

Wash duck and pat dry with paper towels. Rub cavity with salt and pepper. Place it in a roasting pan with celery, garlic, and bay leaves; bake, uncovered, for 35 minutes. Remove from oven; pour off all fat; add wine, capers, and Worcestershire. Return to oven and bake 45 to 60 minutes longer, basting every 15 minutes with a portion of chicken broth. Transfer to a warm serving platter; strain remaining sauce over; cover with thinly sliced truffle and serve. Serves 4 to 6.

QUAILS BRAISED IN WHITE WINE

Quaglie al vino bianco

- 6 tablespoons butter
- 3 slices bacon, chopped
- 6 sage leaves, fresh or dried
- 4 quails, split down the back and spread out flat
- ½ teaspoon salt
- ½ teaspoon white pepper
- ¾ cup dry white wine
- 1 tablespoon flour
- 3 slices white bread, crusts removed, each cut into four triangles, fried in butter

Melt butter in a large skillet; add bacon and sage; add quails, and brown on both sides. Sprinkle with salt and pepper. Stir in wine, cover and cook slowly for 20 to 30 minutes or until quails are tender to touch. Transfer to a warm serving platter; thicken juices remaining in skillet with flour and pour over quails. Arrange fried bread triangles around edge of platter. Serves 6.

LINA'S RABBIT STEW
Coniglio alla Lina

2 3-pound rabbits, fresh or frozen, cut into serving pieces
4 tablespoons butter
2 tablespoons oil
2 carrots, diced
2 stalks celery, diced
1 large onion, sliced
1 clove garlic, chopped
½ teaspoon dried rosemary leaves, if possible fresh
3 bay leaves
4 cloves
1 cup dry white wine
3 tablespoons brandy

Defrost frozen rabbits and dry well. In a large Dutch oven, melt butter; add oil, carrots, celery, onion, garlic, rosemary, bay leaves, and cloves; spoon over rabbit pieces. Over medium heat, cook until vegetables are soft, turning rabbit pieces to brown on both sides. Add wine; cover and simmer for 2 hours. Transfer rabbit pieces to a warm serving platter and keep warm. Force vegetables through a strainer; return to the Dutch oven; add brandy and cook over high heat, stirring constantly, for 2 or 3 minutes. Pour sauce over rabbit pieces, and serve with polenta. Serves 6 to 8.

PAN-BROILED QUAIL OR SQUABS WITH BRANDY

Quaglie in padella o piccioncini al Cognac

6   quails or young squabs
1   teaspoon salt
¼   teaspoon white pepper
6   tablespoons butter
6   sage leaves
¼   pound Italian prosciutto, diced
6   tablespoons brandy

Split quails or squabs down the back and open like a book; wash and dry with paper towels. Sprinkle inside and out with salt and pepper. Heat butter in a large skillet over medium heat; add sage, prosciutto, and quail, skin side down. Place cover on quails with a weight to press them during cooking. Cook for 5 minutes over medium high heat; turn, replace cover and weight; cook 5 minutes longer. Transfer to a warm serving plate and keep warm. Discard fat from skillet, loosen residue stuck to skillet; add brandy and cook over high heat for a few minutes. Pour over quail and serve hot. Serves 4 to 6.

8
Eggs and Cheeses

Uova e Formaggio

Eggs find their way to the Piemontese table in many ways; served hard-cooked with a green herb sauce; fried and pickled; and in the form of a "frittata," the Italian omelet. "Frittata" differs from its French cousin being flat instead of rolled, and the ingredients are beaten with the eggs before cooking. Its virtue is its versatility. Almost any food from cooked meat to vegetables can be added.

Valle d'Aosta, elevated in the northwest corner of Italy amidst such magnificent giants as the Matterhorn and Mont Blanc, is at no loss for scenery. This cheese country is the home of the gentle Fontina, a semi-soft cheese, produced in large wheels, noted for its agreeable flavor and fragrance. Fontina is the main ingredient of "La Fondua," popular around the world. Cheese is always at the Piemontese table at the close of the meal, to be eaten with crisp "grissini," crusty bread, or fruit.

PICKLED FRIED EGGS
Uova fritte sott'aceto

3	tablespoons butter
8	eggs
3	tablespoons oil
1	small onion, sliced
4	fresh or dried sage leaves
¾	cup vinegar
¼	cup water
¼	teaspoon salt
¼	teaspoon white pepper

Melt butter in a frying pan; fry eggs sunny-side-up. Transfer to a deep dish and set aside. In a small saucepan, heat oil; add onion and sage; cook over medium heat until onion is soft; add vinegar, water, salt and pepper; lower heat and simmer for 10 minutes. Pour hot mixture over eggs; cool; refrigerate for 24 hours before serving. Serve chilled. Serves 4.

HARD-COOKED EGGS, ALLA TORINESE
Uova sode, alla Torinese

3	tablespoons butter
2	tablespoons chopped fresh parsley
3	tablespoons chopped fresh basil
½	teaspoon dried rosemary leaves, crumbled
3	tablespoons grated Parmesan cheese
½	teaspoon salt
⅛	teaspoon black pepper
8	hard-cooked eggs, quartered

Melt butter in a small saucepan; add parsley, basil, rosemary, cheese, salt, and pepper; stir and simmer for 10 minutes; set aside to cool. Arrange quartered eggs in a serving dish; pour sauce over. Serve over a slice of toast or a lettuce leaf as an appetizer or a luncheon dish. Serves 4 to 8.

SCRAMBLED EGGS, ASTI-STYLE
Uova strapazzate, all'Astigiana

2	tablespoons butter
2	anchovy fillets, finely chopped
1	tablespoon chopped fresh parsley
½	clove garlic, finely chopped
4	eggs

salt and pepper to taste

Melt butter in a Teflon-coated pan; add anchovy fillets, parsley, and garlic; cook over low heat for 5 minutes. Beat eggs lightly; pour into pan; cook over low heat, stirring constantly until done to your preference. Sprinkle with salt and pepper. Serve hot with toast. Serves 2.

SCRAMBLED EGGS WITH CHEESE
Uova strapazzate, con formaggio

4	eggs
2	tablespoons heavy cream
2	tablespoons grated Parmesan cheese

salt and pepper to taste

2	tablespoons butter

Beat eggs with cream and cheese; add salt and pepper. Melt butter in a Teflon-coated pan; pour in egg mixture. Cook over low heat, stirring constantly, until done to your preference. Serve hot with toast. Serves 2.

SCRAMBLED EGGS WITH TOMATO
Uova strapazzate, con pomodoro

2   tablespoons butter
2   sun-ripened medium tomatoes, peeled and chopped
4   eggs, well beaten
salt and pepper to taste

Melt butter in a Teflon-coated pan; add tomatoes and cook uncovered for 10 minutes. Pour eggs over; cook over low heat, stirring constantly until done to your preference. Season to taste. Serve hot with toast. Serves 2.

FRITTATA (OPEN-FACED ITALIAN OMELET) WITH ONIONS
Frittata di cipolle

The frittata of Piemonte is similar to an omelet, but it differs in two ways: First, it is always flat, not folded, and second, the filling is always mixed in with the eggs. You can use almost anything in a frittata, and it is good eaten hot or cold. Do try one.

3   tablespoons oil
3   medium onions, thinly sliced
6   eggs
1   teaspoon salt
¼   teaspoon white pepper

Use a Teflon-coated 10-inch frying pan, and you will have no problem turning the frittata. Heat oil in frying pan; add onions and cook over medium heat for 6 to 8 minutes, until soft and golden. Beat eggs with salt and pepper; pour over onions; stir and cook over low heat until mixture begins to set. Remove pan from heat, place a plate upside-down over the frittata, and holding plate and pan closely together, turn pan quickly upside-down over the plate. Slip the frittata, cooked side up, from plate into frying pan; and do not stir this time, but cook for 3 or 4 minutes. Slide it back on the plate and serve. Serves 4 to 6.

FRITTATA WITH HERBS
Frittata aromatica

1	cup chopped fresh spinach
2	tablespoons chopped fresh parsley
2	tablespoons chopped fresh basil
3	tablespoons butter
7	eggs
1	teaspoon salt
¼	teaspoon white pepper

Over medium heat, cook spinach, parsley, and basil in butter for 3 or 4 minutes. Proceed as in recipe for Frittata with Onions, page 147. Serves 4 to 6.

GREEN FRITTATA
Frittata verde,
Piemontese

2	cups chopped fresh Swiss chard greens
1	medium onion, sliced thin
1	clove garlic, finely chopped
1	tablespoon chopped fresh parsley
3	tablespoon butter
3	tablespoons grated Parmesan cheese
6	eggs
1	teaspoon salt
¼	teaspoon white pepper

Over medium heat, cook greens, onion, garlic and parsley in butter for 5 minutes; stir in Parmesan cheese. Proceed as in recipe for Frittata with Onions, page 147. Serves 4 to 6.

FRITTATA WITH ASPARAGUS
Frittata di asparagi

1 10-ounce package frozen asparagus spears, thawed and drained
3 tablespoons butter
6 eggs
1 teaspoon salt
¼ teaspoon white pepper

Over medium heat, cook whole asparagus spears in butter for 5 minutes. Proceed as in recipe for Frittata with Onions, page 147. Serves 4 to 6.

FRITTATA WITH TRUFFLE
Frittata Torinese, con tartufi

6 eggs
1 truffle, finely chopped
½ teaspoon salt
⅛ teaspoon nutmeg
3 tablespoons butter

Beat eggs with truffle, salt, and nutmeg. Proceed as in recipe for Frittata with Onions, page 147. Serves 3 to 4.

FRITTATA WITH MUSHROOMS
Frittata di funghi

1 pound fresh mushrooms, sliced
1 clove garlic, finely chopped
1 tablespoon chopped fresh parsley
3 tablespoons butter
6 eggs
1 teaspoon salt
¼ teaspoon white pepper

Over medium heat, cook mushrooms, garlic, and parsley in butter for 5 to 6 minutes, until soft. Proceed as in recipe for Frittata with Onions, page 147. Serves 4 to 6.

FRITTATA WITH ITALIAN SALAMI
Frittata rognosa

6 eggs
½ pound Italian salami, diced
3 tablespoons grated Parmesan cheese
¼ teaspoon salt
3 tablespoons butter

Beat eggs; add salami, cheese, and salt. Proceed as in recipe for Frittata with Onions, page 147. Serves 4 to 6.

PIEMONTESE CHEESE FONDUE
Fonduta alla Piemontese

Why not serve this enticing dish to friends some cold night by the fireplace?

1 pound Fontina cheese, cut into small pieces
1 cup milk
3 tablespoons butter
5 egg yolks
¼ teaspoon white pepper
1 small truffle, very thinly sliced

Place cheese in a bowl; pour milk over; cover and refrigerate for 2 or 3 hours. In an earthenware casserole, over very low heat, melt butter; add cheese and milk; stirring constantly, add egg yolks one by one. Stir until mixture is creamy and smooth; add pepper and truffle. Place casserole over low heat of alcohol burner and keep warm. Do not cook or simmer, just keep warm. Serve with crusty bread cubes for dipping. Serves 6 to 8.

COTTAGE-CHEESE BLEND
Robiola di Rocca-verno, mantecata

Roccaverano is the lilting name of one of the towns famed for the production of Robiola, a soft crumbly cheese of a slightly sweet nature. The word "mantecata" means thoroughly mixed. That is my reason for calling this recipe a cottage-cheese blend.

1 16-ounce container large-curd cottage cheese (not Italian ricotta)
1 clove garlic, forced through a garlic press
3 tablespoons oil
2 tablespoons red wine vinegar
½ teaspoon salt
½ teaspoon white pepper

In a bowl, combine cheese, garlic, oil, vinegar, salt, and pepper. With a fork, mix gently, but thoroughly. Do not use an electric mixer. Cover tightly and refrigerate for 48 hours before serving. This cheese-blend will keep in the refrigerator for 2 weeks. Makes 2 cups.

CHEESE PIE ALLA VALDOSTANA

Crostata alla Valdostana

Preheat over to 450°F.
½ recipe for Egg Pastry (omit sugar, vanilla, and lemon rind), page 186.
1½ pounds Fontina or Gruyère cheese, slivered
3 eggs
½ teaspoon salt
¼ teaspoon white pepper
½ teaspoon nutmeg
1 cup dry white wine

Prepare crust as directed in recipe; bake for 5 minutes. Cool. Arrange slivered cheese over bottom of crust. In a small bowl, beat eggs with salt, pepper, and nutmeg; stir in wine. Pour over cheese in pie shell; bake for 15 minutes; reduce heat to 350°F, and bake 10 minutes longer. Serve hot. Serves 6 to 8.

FONTINA FRITTERS ALLA VALDOSTANA

*Frittelle di fontina,
alla Valdostana*

1½ cups grated Fontina or Swiss cheese
3 tablespoons flour
¼ teaspoon salt
¼ teaspoon white pepper
¼ teaspoon nutmeg
2 eggs
½ cup unflavored breadcrumbs
1 cup oil

In a bowl, combine cheese, flour, salt, pepper, and nutmeg. Beat eggs and add gently to cheese mixture. Shape tablespoons of mixture into 1-inch balls; dip in bread crumbs; shake off excess and flatten lightly. Heat oil to 375°F. in a large skillet; fry fritters, turning once, until golden on both sides. Drain on paper towels. Serve as hors d'oeuvres. Makes about 20 fritters.

9
Vegetables and Salads

Verdure e Insalate

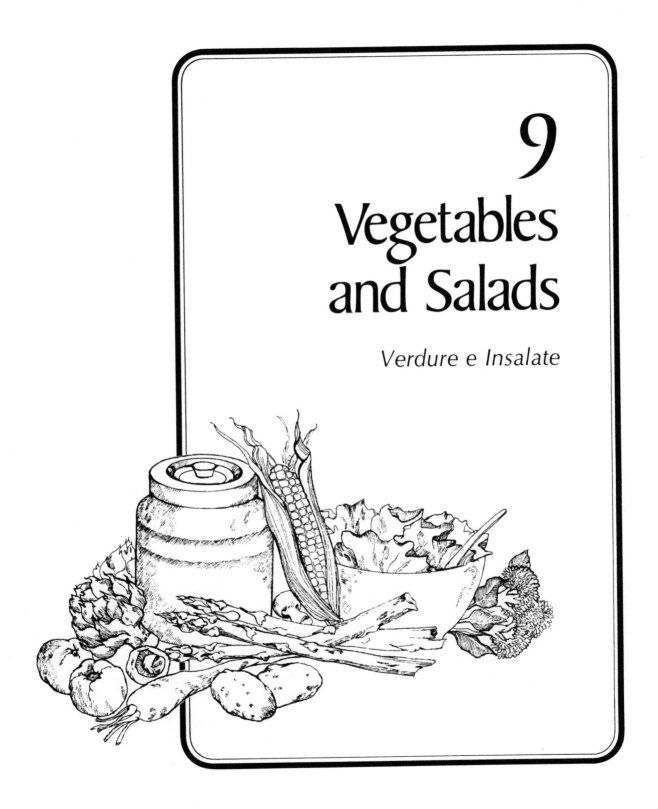

In Piemonte, vegetables are always served as an accompaniment to meat, or chicken. Fresh vegetables are generally used (the frozen ones have not yet become widely popular), this is especially true out in the country, where people grow their own. Wherever you see three square feet of land, you will see vegetables growing. They are cooked in many ways, fried, braised, baked, gratinéed, or simply eaten raw. Mixed salads are also served with the meat course. The most popular is the simplest, just fresh greens with a dressing of oil, vinegar, salt, and pepper. Often salads combining vegetables with rice, seafood, or meat are served as an entrée, a refreshing choice for a hot summer day.

VEGETABLES
Verdure

Time Table for Steaming Vegetables

Artichokes, 18 to 20 minutes
Asparagus, 12 to 15 minutes
Beans, string, whole, 7 to 10 minutes
Beets, sliced, 6 to 8 minutes
Broccoli, 6 to 8 minutes
Brussels sprouts, 12 to 14 minutes
Cabbage, quartered, 15 to 20 minutes
Carrots, sliced, 6 to 8 minutes
Cauliflower, quartered, 12 to 15 minutes
Celery, sliced, 8 to 10 minutes
Corn-on-cob, 5 to 6 minutes
Fennel, sliced, 15 to 20 minutes
Onions, small, 6 to 8 minutes
Potatoes, small, 14 to 20 minutes
Spinach, 8 to 10 minutes
Zucchini, sliced, 5 to 7 minutes

STUFFED ARTICHOKES ALLA TORINESE

Carciofi ripieni alla Torinese

Preheat oven to 350°F.

6 medium artichokes
juice of one lemon
1 cup coarsely chopped roast beef
6 thin slices cooked ham, coarsely chopped
3 tablespoons chopped fresh parsley
1 egg, beaten
1 teaspoon salt
½ teaspoon black pepper
3 tablespoons butter
1 cup dry white wine
½ cup water
2 beef-bouillon cubes, crushed

Wash artichokes; remove and discard outer leaves. Cut in half lengthwise and remove choke. Rub with lemon juice; place in steam basket and steam over one inch of salted water for 18 to 20 minutes. Drain and set aside. In a bowl, combine beef, ham, parsley, egg, salt, and pepper; mix well. Fill artichokes with mixture and arrange in one layer in a shallow baking pan; dot with butter; pour wine and water into pan; add bouillon cubes; cover with foil and bake for 1 hour. Transfer very gently to a warm serving dish and serve hot. Serves 6.

SCRUMPTIOUS ASPARAGUS

Asparagi saporiti

2 pounds fresh asparagus, or 2 10-ounce packages frozen asparagus spears
6 anchovy fillets
½ clove garlic
3 sprigs fresh parsley
6 tablespoons butter
⅛ teaspoon white pepper
juice of one lemon

Clean fresh asparagus and cook in salted water for 10 to 15 minutes, until just tender. Cook frozen asparagus in boiling salted water for 5 minutes. Combine anchovy fillets, garlic, and parsley; chop very fine. Melt butter in a small saucepan; add chopped mixture and pepper; cook over low heat for 10 minutes. Drain asparagus thoroughly; transfer to a warm serving dish; pour sauce over; sprinkle with lemon juice and serve immediately. Serves 4 to 6.

COLD ASPARAGUS WITH TUNA FISH
Asparagi freddi, con tonno

The bountiful asparagus of Piemonte is grown in the regions around the towns of Santena, Poirino, and Cambiano. It is dark green, and large in size, with exceptional flavor. *"La festa degli asparagi,"* the asparagus festival, is a pageant that no asparagus-loving Torinese would choose to miss; I remember it lasted for 3 days in the springtime. One could sample asparagus prepared just about every way that is possible.

1½ cups Mayonnaise Sauce, ½ recipe, page 69
 2 pounds fresh asparagus, or 2 10-ounce packages frozen asparagus spears
 1 6½-ounce can tuna fish, drained
 1 small onion, cut in quarters
 4 capers
 4 anchovy fillets
 2 tablespoons chopped fresh parsley

Make mayonnaise and set aside. Cook fresh asparagus in boiling salted water for 10 to 15 minutes, until just tender. Thaw and drain frozen asparagus. In the blender container combine tuna, onion, capers, and anchovy fillets; chop fine. Add mayonnaise and parsley and blend at low speed until well mixed. Arrange asparagus in a deep serving dish; pour sauce over; set aside for two hours before serving. Keep in cool place, but do not refrigerate. Serves 4 to 6.

SAUTÉED ASPARAGUS
Asparagi fritti

3 pounds fresh asparagus, green part only
½ cup flour
2 eggs, beaten
1 cup unflavored bread crumbs
4 tablespoons grated Parmesan cheese
3 tablespoons butter
3 tablespoons oil
1 teaspoon salt
¼ teaspoon white pepper

Wash and dry asparagus. Dip each spear into flour, then into eggs and then into bread crumbs combined with cheese. Melt butter in a frying pan; add oil and sauté asparagus for 10 minutes, until tender. Transfer to a warm serving dish, sprinkle with salt and pepper and serve hot. Serves 6.

ASPARAGUS WITH BUTTER AND CHEESE
Asparagi al burro e formaggio

2 pounds fresh asparagus, or
2 10-ounce packages frozen asparagus spears
6 tablespoons butter, melted
½ cup grated Parmesan cheese

Clean fresh asparagus and cook in salted water for 10 to 15 minutes. Cook frozen asparagus in salted water for 5 minutes. Drain. Arrange asparagus with tips toward center, on a warm round serving platter. Pour over the melted butter and sprinkle with cheese. Serves 4 to 6.

SWEET AND SOUR GREEN BEANS
Fagiolini in salsa agrodolce

2 pounds fresh green beans
2 tablespoons sugar
¼ cup wine vinegar
2 egg yolks
¼ cup water

Remove ends and string from beans. Leave whole. Steam for 7 to 10 minutes; drain and keep warm. In a small saucepan, combine sugar, vinegar, egg yolks, and water; cook over low heat, stirring constantly, until sauce is thickened and smooth; do not boil. Transfer beans to a serving dish; pour sauce over and serve hot. Serves 6.

CARROT BALLS
Palline di carote

Serve this unusual dish as the vegetable of a meal or as an hors d'oeuvre.

    1   cup flour
    ½   teaspoon salt
    ¼   teaspoon white pepper
    1½ teaspoons baking powder
    4   tablespoons butter
    ¾   cup grated carrots
oil for deep frying

In a bowl, combine flour, salt, pepper, baking powder, and butter; with a fork, work into a crumbling mixture. Add carrots and enough water to make a fairly stiff dough. Flour your hands. Using 1 teaspoon of dough at a time, roll into balls the size of a small walnut. Heat oil and fry, a few at a time, for 3 to 4 minutes, until crisp. Serve hot. Serves 4 to 6.

BAKED CAULI-FLOWER ALLA PIEMONTESE
Cavolfiore al forno alla Piemontese

Preheat oven to 400°F.
    1   medium cauliflower
    4   tablespoons butter
    2   whole cloves garlic, slightly crushed
    ¼   cup unflavored bread crumbs
    ½   cup shredded Fontina or Swiss cheese

Trim cauliflower, removing outer leaves and core; break into flowerets. Place in a steam basket and steam over 1 inch of salted water for 12 minutes, until tender-firm; drain. Transfer to a bake-and-serve dish and set aside. In a small saucepan, melt butter; sauté garlic for 5 minutes; discard garlic; add bread crumbs to butter and sauté 5 minutes. Pour over cauliflower; sprinkle with cheese and bake for 15 minutes. Serves 6.

BREADED FRIED CAULIFLOWER
Cavolfiore panato, fritto

1	medium head of cauliflower, separated into flowerets
½	cup flour
2	eggs, well beaten
1¼	cups unflavored bread crumbs
1	cup oil
½	teaspoon salt

Place flowerets in steam basket and steam over 1-inch salted water for 10 minutes; drain and cool. Dip each floweret into flour; shake off excess; dip into eggs, then into bread crumbs; shake off excess. Refrigerate for 1 hour. Heat oil in a large skillet and fry cauliflower until golden; drain on paper towels. Transfer to a warm serving dish; sprinkle with salt and serve hot. Serves 6.

SWEET AND SOUR EGGPLANT
Melanzane agrodolce

Another interesting suggestion for either hors d'oeuvre or vegetable course. Serve with toothpicks.

1	large eggplant, about 1 pound
1	cup oil
6	tablespoons sugar
½	cup lemon juice, or white vinegar
1	tablespoon tomato paste

Peel eggplant, cut lengthwise, slice across, then cut into 4 × ½-inch sticks. Fry eggplant sticks in hot oil, a few at a time, until golden brown. Drain on paper towels. Transfer to a warm serving dish and keep warm. In a small saucepan, melt sugar (do not allow to burn); add lemon juice and tomato paste; stir and simmer for 2 or 3 minutes. Pour over eggplant sticks and serve hot. Serves 4 to 6.

BAKED EGG-PLANT ALLA TORINESE

Melanzane gratinate, alla Torinese

Preheat oven to 400°F.

4	tablespoons butter
1	medium onion, finely chopped
1	clove garlic, finely chopped
2½	tablespoons flour
1½	cups water
2	chicken-bouillon cubes, crumbled
3	canned plum tomatoes, chopped
½	teaspoon dried marjoram, crumbled
½	teaspoon salt
½	teaspoon white pepper
2	large eggplants, peeled and cut across into ¼-inch thick slices
½	cup flour
1	cup oil
¼	pound Fontina cheese, thinly sliced

Melt butter in a small saucepan; add onion and garlic; sauté until golden. Add flour; stir a few minutes (do not allow flour to burn). Remove saucepan from heat; stir in water and bouillon cubes; stir until well mixed. Return saucepan to heat; stir until sauce thickens; add tomatoes, marjoram, salt, and pepper. Cover, simmer over low heat for 10 minutes, stirring constantly. Set aside. Coat eggplant slices with flour; heat oil in skillet and fry slices gently until golden brown. Arrange in alternating layers with sauce in a bake-and-serve dish, ending with a top layer of sauce; arrange cheese over sauce; bake until cheese is melted. Serve hot. Serves 6.

FRIED EGGPLANT
Melanzane fritte

1 large eggplant, about 1 pound
1 cup flour
¾ cup cold water
2 eggs, beaten
oil
1 tablespoon brandy

Peel eggplant; cut into 4 × ½-inch sticks. In a bowl, combine flour, water, eggs, ¼ cup oil, and brandy; beat to a smooth batter. Heat 1 inch of oil in a frying pan; dip eggplant sticks into batter, allow excess batter to drain off; fry, a few sticks at a time, for 2 or 3 minutes, until golden. Drain on paper towels. Serve hot. Serves 6. Serves 8 to 12 as hors d'oeuvre.

LEEKS AND HAM CASSEROLE
Porri e prosciutto, al forno

Preheat oven to 400°F.
8 leeks
8 thin slices of Italian prosciutto
4 tablespoons butter
2 tablespoons flour
1½ cups milk, heated
½ cup grated Parmesan cheese
¼ teaspoon salt
¼ teaspoon white pepper

Trim root and tops of greens from leeks. Wash and cook in boiling salted water for 10 minutes. Drain, and wrap each leek with a slice of prosciutto. Arrange on a bake-and-serve dish and set aside. In a small saucepan, melt butter; blend in flour, stirring constantly with a wooden spoon, for 2 or 3 minutes. Remove from heat and add hot milk, a little at a time, continuing to stir. Return to low heat; cook, stirring, until creamy and smooth. Blend in cheese, salt, and pepper. Pour sauce over leeks. Bake for 15 minutes. Serves 4.

BAKED FENNELS
Finocchi al forno

Preheat oven to 400°F.

4 fennels
2 chicken-bouillon cubes
½ cup hot water
5 tablespoons butter
2 tablespoons chopped fresh parsley
3 tablespoons unflavored bread crumbs

Cut fennels into halves; wash and place in a steam basket; steam over 1-inch salted water for 15 to 20 minutes, until fork tender. Drain and transfer to a buttered bake-and-serve dish. Dissolve bouillon cubes in hot water; pour into dish around base of fennels; dot with butter; sprinkle with parsley and bread crumbs, and bake for 15 minutes. Serve hot. Serves 6.

MUSHROOM TART
Crostata di funghi

Preheat oven to 400°F.

1 recipe Egg Pastry, page 186. Omit sugar, vanilla and lemon rind
6 tablespoons butter
2 pounds fresh mushrooms, washed and sliced
1 tablespoon flour
½ cup dry white wine
1 teaspoon salt
½ teaspoon white pepper
½ cup homemade or canned beef broth, heated
2 egg yolks

Make dough for pastry and refrigerate until ready for use. Divide dough in two. Roll one half on a lightly floured surface into a 12-inch circle, ⅛-inch thick; gently transfer to a buttered and floured 10-inch fluted pie pan. Prick bottom of dough with a fork; bake for 10 minutes. Remove from oven and set aside. In a skillet, over medium heat, melt 3 tablespoons butter; sauté mushrooms for 5 minutes, stir in flour; add wine, salt, pepper, broth, and egg yolks. Stir well, return to low heat and cook, stirring for 10 minutes. Pour mushrooms into baked shells. Roll out second half of pastry. Cut in narrow strips; weave in lattice fashion over tart. Trim ends. Moisten edge of bottom crust. With fingers, press down strips at edge. Bake for 10 minutes. Serve hot as a luncheon or hors d'oeuvre dish. Serves 6 to 8.

MUSHROOMS WITH WHITE WINE
Funghi al vino bianco

4	tablespoons butter
⅓	cup dry white wine
1	tablespoon lemon juice
1	small onion, finely chopped
1	tablespoon tomato paste
1	bay leaf
½	teaspoon salt
¼	teaspoon white pepper
1	pound fresh mushrooms, cut into quarters

Put all ingredients except mushrooms in a saucepan, cover, and simmer for 5 minutes. Add mushrooms and simmer for 10 minutes. Remove mushrooms from saucepan with a slotted spoon and transfer to a warm serving bowl. Turn heat to high; boil sauce rapidly and stir until liquid has the consistency of syrup; remove bay leaf; pour sauce over mushrooms and serve hot. Serves 4.

BREADED FRIED MUSHROOMS
Funghi panati fritti

1½	pounds fresh mushrooms
2	eggs, well beaten
1½	cups unflavored breadcrumbs
1	cup oil
½	teaspoon salt
¼	teaspoon white pepper

Clean mushrooms, wash and pat dry; quarter lengthwise; dip into eggs, then into breadcrumbs; shake off excess. Refrigerate for 1 hour. In skillet, heat oil over medium-high heat; fry mushrooms until golden; drain on paper towels. Transfer to a warm serving dish; sprinkle with salt and pepper; serve hot. Serves 6.

STUFFED BAKED ONIONS
Cipolle ripiene al forno

Preheat oven to 350°F.
- 6 large onions
- 3 tablespoons butter
- 1 cup chopped cooked meat
- 4 tablespoons grated Parmesan cheese
- 3 tablespoons unflavored bread crumbs
- 1 tablespoon brandy
- ½ teaspoon salt
- ¼ teaspoon white pepper

Peel onions; scoop out centers leaving shells. Chop scooped out pulp fine and sauté for 5 minutes in 2 tablespoons butter. In a bowl, combine sautéed onions, meat, cheese, bread crumbs, brandy, salt, and pepper; mix well. Fill onion shells with mixture; dot with remaining 1 tablespoon butter; place in a baking dish; cover with foil and bake for 30 minutes. Transfer to a warm serving dish and serve hot. Serves 6.

BAKED STUFFED ONION, SETTIMO-STYLE
Cipolle ripiene al forno alla Settimese

On the last Saturday in August, the villagers of Settimo, near Torino, celebrate the festival of their Patron Saint. This ancient recipe is the traditional dish of the day. It is served hot or cold.

Preheat oven to 350°F.
- 8 medium onions
- 2 slices soft white bread, crusts removed
- ½ cup milk
- 2 hard-cooked egg yolks, crumbled
- 6 amaretti (Italian macaroons) crumbled
- 3 tablespoons grated Parmesan cheese
- ⅛ teaspoon cloves
- ⅛ teaspoon cinnamon
- ⅛ teaspoon white pepper
- 2 whole eggs, beaten
- 4 tablespoons butter

Peel onions; place in saucepan with salted water to cover; boil for 15 minutes. Drain and cut onions in half; remove cores and shape outer leaves to form a cup. Set aside. Soak bread in milk for a few minutes; squeeze dry, crumble, and place in a bowl. Add hard-cooked egg yolks, amaretti, cheese, clove, cinnamon, pepper, and eggs, and mix well. Fill onion cups; dot with butter. Place in a baking dish and bake for 30 minutes. Serves 6 to 8.

POTATOES ALLA VALDOSTANA
Patate alla Valdostana

6	medium potatoes
½	cup chopped onions
6	tablespoons butter
1	cup shredded Fontina cheese
½	teaspoon salt
½	teaspoon white pepper

Peel potatoes and steam over 1 inch salted water for 20 minutes. Drain and cool. Force potatoes through a potato ricer into a bowl. Sauté chopped onions in 2 tablespoons butter for 5 minutes, until soft; combine potatoes, onions, cheese, salt, and pepper; mix well. Melt remaining 4 tablespoons butter in a Teflon-coated skillet; pat potato mixture evenly over bottom. Cover and cook over medium heat for 8 to 10 minutes, until underside is golden brown. Place a plate, upside-down, over potatoes and holding plate and pan closely together, turn pan quickly so potatoes drop on plate. Slip potatoes brown side up from plate to pan and brown other side. Serves 6.

POTATO PATTIES ALLA CANAVESANA
Frittelle di patate alla Canavesana

2	pounds potatoes, unpeeled
4	eggs
½	cup sugar
½	teaspoon salt
	grated rind and juice of one lemon
½	cup flour
6	tablespoons butter

Cook potatoes in salted water to cover for 30 minutes, until soft. Drain, cool, peel, and force through a potato ricer into a bowl; cool completely. Add eggs, one at a time, stirring, but not beating. Add sugar, salt, lemon juice and rind; blend well. Form mixture into patties; dip into flour on both sides; shake off excess. Melt butter in a large frying pan; cook patties gently until golden brown, turning once. Serves 6.

POTATOES SAVOY-STYLE
Patate alla Savoiarda

Preheat oven to 350°F.

1 pound baking potatoes
¾ cup grated Gruyère or Swiss cheese
¼ cup grated Parmesan cheese
⅔ cup homemade or canned beef broth
¼ teaspoon salt
¼ teaspoon white pepper
4 tablespoons butter

Peel, thinly slice and soak potatoes in cold water for 10 minutes; drain and dry with paper towels. In a buttered 9-inch pie plate, arrange a layer of potatoes; sprinkle with a portion of cheeses. Arrange three or four more layers of potatoes and cheeses, ending with cheeses. Pour over beef broth; sprinkle with salt and pepper; dot with butter and bake for 30 to 40 minutes, until potatoes are tender and browned. Serves 4 to 6.

SMALL BUTTER POTATOES
Patatine al burro

One of the signs of spring (yes, spring) in the vegetable markets of Piemonte are basketsful of very small golden potatoes. They look like unshelled peanuts, and are called *patatine del burro*, meaning "small, butter potatoes," because their flavor resembles butter. These potato-ettes are delicious with roasted meats. Since I have not been able to find them in the United States, I now make the dish with regular potatoes shaped into balls with a melon-ball cutter.

6 large baking potatoes, peeled
½ cup butter
½ teaspoon rosemary leaves, crumbled
1 whole clove garlic
salt

Using a melon-ball cutter, cut raw potatoes into balls. Use remaining pieces of potatoes to make potato soup. Soak potato balls in cold water for 30 minutes; drain, and dry with paper towels. In a large frying pan, heat butter with rosemary and garlic; add potatoes; shaking pan frequently, brown them evenly. Discard garlic. Transfer to a warm serving dish; sprinkle with salt and serve. Serves 6 to 8.

ITALIAN MASHED POTATOES
Purée di patate

With a difference!

2 pounds potatoes, unpeeled
6 tablespoons butter
¾ cup milk, heated
½ cup grated Parmesan cheese
2 egg yolks
1 teaspoon salt
¼ teaspoon white pepper
¼ teaspoon nutmeg

Cook potatoes in boiling salted water for 30 minutes, until tender; drain and peel while hot. Melt butter in a stainless steel saucepan over low heat; force potatoes through a potato-ricer directly over butter in saucepan. Mix at low speed with an electric mixer as you add hot milk, a little at a time, always mixing; mix in cheese, egg yolks, salt, pepper, and nutmeg. Potatoes should be soft and fluffy; if necessary, add more hot milk. Serve immediately. Serves 6 to 8.

POTATO AND SPINACH ROLL

Rotolo di patate e spinaci

2 pounds potatoes, peeled and diced
2 pounds fresh spinach, or
2 10-ounce packages frozen chopped spinach
1 cup flour
2 eggs
2 teaspoons salt
½ teaspoon white pepper
4 tablespoons butter
1 teaspoon dried sage leaves, crumbled
½ cup grated Parmesan cheese

Cook potatoes in boiling, salted water for 20 minutes, until tender. Drain and force through a potato ricer onto a floured pastry board. Cool. Boil fresh spinach for fifteen minutes; frozen spinach for five minutes. Drain thoroughly and cool. Add spinach to potatoes; add flour, eggs, 1 teaspoon salt, and pepper; mix well with your hands. Shape mixture into a roll; wrap it tightly with cheese cloth; tie ends with string. In a large kettle, heat 4 quarts of water to boiling; add remaining 1 teaspoon salt; immerse roll and cook gently for 15 minutes. Remove from water, unwrap and cool for a few minutes. Meanwhile, in a small saucepan melt butter, add sage and simmer for 10 minutes; strain, and discard sage leaves. Cut roll into 1-inch slices; arrange on a warm serving dish; pour butter over. Sprinkle with cheese and serve hot. Serves 6 to 8.

STUFFED BAKED TOMATO

Pomodori ripieni, al forno

Preheat oven to 350°F.

6 large, or 12 small, tomatoes
1 10-ounce package frozen chopped spinach
3 tablespoons melted butter
6 tablespoons grated Parmesan cheese
2 eggs, beaten
½ teaspoon salt
2 hard-cooked egg yolks, sieved

Remove ½ inch from top of each tomato; scoop out pulp and seeds (use for a sauce). Thaw spinach and drain well. In a bowl combine spinach, butter, cheese, eggs, and salt, and mix well. Fill tomato with spinach mixture. Place in a baking dish and bake for 30 minutes. Remove from oven; transfer to a serving dish; garnish tomatoes with sieved egg yolks, and serve hot. Serves 6.

SPINACH TART
Crostata di spinaci

Preheat oven to 400°F.

1 recipe Egg Pastry, page 186. Omit sugar, vanilla and lemon rind
3 tablespoons butter
½ cup chopped onions
2 pounds fresh spinach or 2 10-ounce packages frozen spinach leaves
4 tablespoons grated Parmesan cheese
1 teaspoon salt

Melt butter in a saucepan; add onions and cook until tender; add washed, trimmed and cooked spinach, cheese, and salt; cook for 5 minutes. Proceed as in recipe for Mushroom Tart, page 163. Serve hot. Serves 6.

FRIED ZUCCHINI
Zucchine fritte

1 pound small firm zucchini
1 cup flour
¾ cup cold water
2 eggs, beaten
¼ cup oil
1 tablespoon brandy
oil for frying

Wash zucchini and cut into 4 × ½-inch sticks. In a bowl, combine flour, water, eggs, oil, and brandy; beat to a smooth batter. Heat oil in a frying pan; dip zucchini into batter; allow excess batter to drain off, and fry, a few at a time, for 2 or 3 minutes, until golden. Drain on paper towels. Serve hot. Serves 6.

FRIED ZUCCHINI WITH ALMONDS
Zucchine fritte con mandorle

1½   pounds fresh zucchini, about 6 to 8-inches long
2   tablespoons oil
2   tablespoons butter
¼   cup dry white wine
2   tablespoons lemon juice
½   teaspoon salt
½   cup slivered almonds

Wash and cut zucchini into ¼-inch slices; sauté slices in oil and butter for 5 minutes, stirring frequently. Add wine, lemon juice, and salt; simmer for 5 minutes; add almonds and simmer 5 minutes longer. Transfer to a warm serving dish and serve hot. Serves 6.

GRAND-MOTHER'S STUFFED ZUCCHINI
Zucchine ripiene, della Nonna

Preheat oven to 400°F.

10   fresh zucchini, about 1½ to 2 inches in diameter
3   tablespoons butter
1   large onion, sliced
4   tablespoons flour
1   cup milk, heated
½   cup grated Parmesan cheese
2   tablespoons chopped fresh parsley
½   teaspoon salt
¼   teaspoon nutmeg
5   amaretti (Italian macaroons) crumbled
5   egg yolks

Wash zucchini under cold water; cut off and discard both ends; cut crosswise into 2-inch sections; with vegetable corer, remove all pulp; be careful not to perforate outside skin. Chop pulp and set aside. Simmer hollowed-out zucchini in boiling salted water for 15 minutes. Drain and set aside. In a saucepan, melt butter, add onion, cook over medium heat until onion turns golden; remove from saucepan. To butter remaining in saucepan, add flour and stir for 2 minutes; add hot milk and stir constantly, until sauce is creamy and thickened; mix in cheese, parsley, salt, nutmeg, amaretti, and egg yolks. Stuff hollowed-out zucchini with the mixture; arrange in a buttered bake-and-serve dish; bake for 20 to 30 minutes. Serve hot or cold. Serves 6.

MARINATED ZUCCHINI
Zucchine sott'aceto

2 pounds fresh zucchini
1 cup oil
1 medium onion, sliced
1 stalk celery, cut into 1-inch pieces
2 cloves garlic, sliced
1 teaspoon salt
½ teaspoon white pepper
2 cups white vinegar
1 cup water

Wash zucchini in cold water; cut off and discard both ends; cut into 2-inch strips, ½ inch thick. In a skillet, deep-fry strips in hot oil for 2 minutes. Remove to a deep bowl. To prepare marinade, pour off all but ½ cup oil from skillet; sauté onion, celery, and garlic for 10 minutes. Add salt, pepper, vinegar and water and simmer for 15 minutes. Pour marinade, while hot, over zucchini; cool and refrigerate for 48 hours before serving. Marinated Zucchini will keep in refrigerator for one week. Serves 6.

MIXED VEGE-TABLES ALLA MONFERRINA
Verdure miste, alla Monferrina

3 tablespoons butter
3 tablespoons oil
1 pound onions, sliced
3 medium zucchini, cut in ¼-inch slices
3 green peppers, cut into ½-inch strips
2 stalks celery, cut into 2-inch pieces
3 large sun-ripened tomatoes, or 4 canned plum tomatoes, chopped
1 teaspoon salt
½ teaspoon black pepper
4 leaves fresh basil

Melt butter in a large skillet; add oil; sauté onions for 5 minutes; add remaining vegetables, salt, pepper, and basil. Cover and cook over low heat for 30 minutes. Uncover and continue to cook for 15 minutes. Transfer to a warm deep serving dish and serve hot. Serves 6.

SALADS
Insalate

GREEN BEAN SALAD ALLA PIEMONTESE
Insalata di fagiolini, alla Piemontese

1 pound fresh green beans, cut into 2-inch pieces
3 tablespoons oil
1 tablespoon wine vinegar
½ teaspoon salt
¼ teaspoon white pepper
1 clove garlic, finely chopped
1 tablespoon chopped fresh parsley
1 tablespoon chopped fresh basil

In a steam basket, steam beans over 1 inch salted water for 7 to 10 minutes until tender; drain and cool. Transfer to a salad bowl. In a small bowl, mix oil, vinegar, salt, pepper, garlic, parsley, and basil; pour over the beans; toss and place in the refrigerator for 1 hour before serving. Serves 4 to 6.

BEAN SALAD WITH GREEN MAYONNAISE
Insalata di fagioli, con maionese verde

1 16-ounce can red kidney beans
1 16-ounce can white kidney beans
1 clove garlic, finely chopped
1 cup Green Mayonnaise, recipe page 69

Drain and rinse beans; drain again; transfer to a salad bowl; add garlic and mayonnaise. Toss gently but thoroughly. Serve at room temperature. Serves 6 to 8.

RED CABBAGE SALAD, WITH BAGNA CAÔDA
Insalata di cavolo rosso, con bagna caôda

1 large head of red cabbage
1 recipe Bagna Caôda, page 6
4 tablespoons red wine vinegar

Remove and discard outer leaves and core of cabbage. Coarsely shred remaining cabbage. Wash thoroughly and drain well. Transfer into a large salad bowl. Prepare Bagna Caôda, stir in vinegar, and pour over cabbage while still hot; toss gently. It is very good eaten warm, but it is also delicious cold. Salad will keep in refrigerator for two or three days. Serves 6 to 10.

GRANDFATHER ANTONIO'S SALAD
Insalata di Nonno Antonio

2 bunches escarole lettuce, white parts only
1 clove garlic
1 egg
3 tablespoons oil
1 tablespoon wine vinegar
⅛ teaspoon white pepper
4 anchovy fillets, cut into ½-inch pieces
salt to taste

Wash lettuce and drain well; tear leaves into bite-size pieces by hand; set aside. Rub bottom of salad bowl with cut clove of garlic, add egg and beat well; vigorously mix in oil, vinegar, and pepper. Add lettuce and anchovy fillets; toss gently, but thoroughly. Add salt to taste. Serve immediately. Serves 4 to 6.

RAW PEA SALAD WITH EGGS
Insalata di piselli freschi e uova

lettuce leaves
1 pound fresh peas, shelled
4 hard-cooked eggs, chopped
2 tablespoons oil
1 tablespoon wine vinegar
½ teaspoon salt
¼ teaspoon white pepper

Arrange lettuce leaves in individual salad bowls; divide raw peas into bowls; top with a portion of hard-cooked eggs. Combine oil, vinegar, salt, and pepper in a small bowl; blend well. Just before serving, sprinkle some of the dressing over each bowl. Serves 6.

DANDELION SALAD
Insalata di girasoli

One good way to remove the dandelions from your lawn is to eat them in a salad. They are a rich souce of Vitamin A, which is very good for your eyes. Pick the choice young greens in the springtime.

1	pound of young dandelion greens
3	tablespoons oil
1	tablespoon wine vinegar
¼	teaspoon salt
½	teaspoon pepper
2	hard-cooked eggs, chopped
1	clove garlic, finely chopped
4	anchovy fillets, chopped

Remove roots and tough stems from dandelions; wash in several changes of water. Drain in a clean cloth. Place in a large salad bowl. In a small bowl combine oil, vinegar, salt, pepper, eggs, garlic, and anchovy fillets; mix well. Pour over dandelions; toss and serve immediately. Serves 4 to 6.

POTATO SALAD WITH BEER ALLA VALDOSTANA
Insalata di patate, alla Valdostana

5	large baking potatoes
½	cup beer
3	tablespoons chopped fresh parsley
1	small onion, thinly sliced
3	tablespoons oil
1	tablespoon wine vinegar
1	tablespoon Dijon mustard

Wash unpeeled potatoes and boil in salted water for 30 minutes, or until tender but firm. Drain, peel, and slice into ¼-inch thick slices. Put potatoes in a salad bowl; pour beer over; stir gently and let them absorb the beer. Add parsley, onion, oil, vinegar, and mustard; mix well and serve at room temperature. Serve 6.

RICE AND POTATO SALAD SIGNOR ANTONIO

Insalata di riso e patate, Signor Antonio

6	tablespoons oil
2	tablespoons wine vinegar
1	teaspoon Dijon mustard
½	teaspoon salt
1	tablespoon finely chopped fresh parsley
3	large potatoes, boiled, peeled, and thinly sliced
1½	cups cooked rice
1	head escarole lettuce, white parts only, torn by hand into bite-size pieces
2	6½-ounce cans tuna fish, drained and flaked
3	sun-ripened tomatoes, sliced
2	sweet red or yellow peppers, cut into matchstick-strips
3	hard-cooked eggs, thinly sliced
2	2-ounce cans anchovy fillets, cut into pieces
1	medium-size yellow sweet onion, sliced thin
½	cup black olives, pitted, cut in half

In a small bowl mix oil, vinegar, mustard, salt, and parsley. In a glass salad bowl, arrange potatoes in one layer; top with the rice; sprinkle with 2 tablespoons dressing; add the escarole; center a mound of tuna fish on top. Garnish with tomatoes, peppers, eggs, anchovy fillets, onions, and olives. Pour over remaining dressing and serve immediately. Serves 6 to 8.

TOMATO SALAD
Insalata di pomodoro

6 medium sun-ripened tomatoes
3 hard-cooked eggs, diced
2 bunches green onions, scallions, sliced
5 tablespoons oil
3 tablespoons wine vinegar
2 tablespoons chopped fresh parsley
2 tablespoons chopped fresh basil
1 teaspoon salt
¼ teaspoon black pepper

If you prefer, you can peel the tomatoes, but it is not necessary. Slice them into a salad bowl; add eggs and scallions; combine oil and vinegar and pour over; sprinkle with parsley, basil, salt, and pepper. Toss gently; cover and refrigerate for two or three hours. Serve chilled. Serves 6.

HERBED VINEGAR

To add special flavor to your salads, make your own garden vinegars.

BASIL AND GARLIC VINEGAR
Aceto al basilico e aglio

1 cup fresh basil leaves
1 quart wine vinegar or white vinegar
4 cloves garlic, cut in half

Wash basil leaves and pat dry with paper towels. Remove some of the vinegar from bottle. Push in basil leaves and garlic. Fill with vinegar. Close bottle tightly and keep in cool place for at least one month before using. When ready to use do not remove basil and garlic from bottle; refill with more vinegar. This is especially good with fresh tomatoes or string bean salads.

Other Herbed Vinegars: Use these herbs in vinegar: tarragon, oregano, marjoram, and thyme. Prepare as above, using ½ cup of fresh herbs to each quart of vinegar.

10
Desserts
and Fruits

Dolci e Frutta

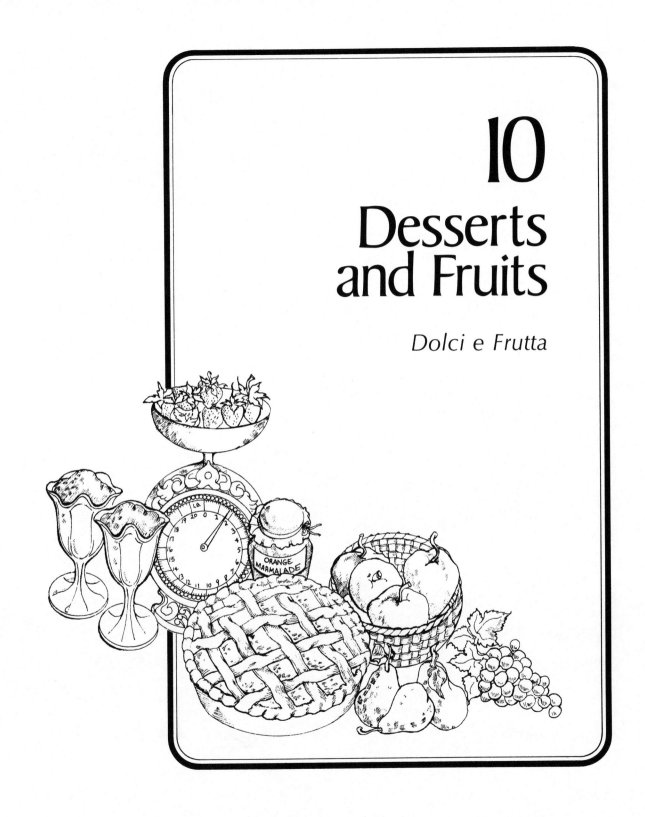

This is a chapter of secret formulas. Not that the recipes are unfamiliar, but that here, arcane methods are disclosed that are usually privy to professional chefs. Perhaps it's the toddy of rum in the *dolce freddo*, the grated lemon rind in the Egg Pastry, measuring the ingredients in egg shells for "Zabaione," or the exotic additions of apricots to the fruit-pie fillings. Touches such as these balance the difference between a good dessert and a great dessert.

The orchards and fruit gardens of Piemonte produce luscious harvests, so it is natural that the favorite desserts of the Piemontese are made with fruit. Stuffed and baked fruit, fresh fruits with luscious creams, or fruit baked in wine and liqueurs, are persona grata on the sweet menu.

CHILLED DESSERT, TERESA'S WAY
Zuppa inglese, Teresa

1	recipe for Zabaione, page 183
2/3	cup heavy cream
36	ladyfingers
1½	cups Port wine
12	red and 12 green candied cherries

Cool zabaione. Whip cream and fold into zabaione. One by one, dip ladyfingers very quickly into port wine; arrange a layer in a serving plate and carefully spread a portion of zabaione-cream mixture over. Repeat for 3 or 4 layers, ending with a top layer of cream. Decorate with cherries. Cover and refrigerate for 24 hours before serving. Serves 8 to 12.

ORANGE-APRICOT SORBET
Sorbetto d'arance a albicocche

½	cup sugar
1	cup water, heated
	grated rind of one orange
	juice of four oranges
6	apricots, fresh or canned, mashed

Dissolve sugar in hot water; cool. Stir in orange rind and juice and apricots; mix well. Pour into 1 or 2 freezer trays and freeze for at least 3 hours. Remove from trays and place in a chilled bowl and beat with rotary beater until smooth. Pour into sherbet glasses and return to freezer until serving time. Serves 4 to 6.

STRAWBERRIES WITH MARSALA OR PORT WINE
Fragole al Marsala o Porto

1 quart fresh strawberries
¾ cup sweet Marsala or Port wine
2 tablespoons fresh lemon juice
3 tablespoons sugar

Wash, slice, and drain strawberries. Place in a serving bowl; pour wine and lemon juice over. Sprinkle with sugar; mix well; cover and chill. Serves 6.

PEACHES WITH MARSALA OR PORT WINE
Pesche al Marsala o Porto

6 large fresh peaches
¾ cup dry Marsala or Port wine
3 tablespoons sugar
¼ teaspoon cinnamon

Peel peaches and slice into a serving bowl. Pour wine over; sprinkle with sugar and cinnamon. Mix well and serve at room temperature. Serves 6.

COFFEE SORBET
Sorbetto di caffé

A cool and light dessert for summer meals.

2½ cups very strong Italian coffee, hot
¼ cup sugar

Combine coffee with sugar and stir until sugar has dissolved. Pour into 1 or 2 freezer trays; store in freezer for at least 3 hours. Remove from tray and place in a chilled bowl; beat with rotary beater until smooth. Pour into sherbet glasses and return to freezer until serving time. Serves 4 to 6.

ZABAIONE
Zabaione

The origin of this dessert goes back to the early 1800s, to the Court of Vittorio Emanuele I, then in Torino. It is easy to make, if you measure by egg shells and use a double-boiler for the preparation.

2 egg yolks
6 half egg shells of sugar
6 half egg shells of dry Marsala or Port wine
dash of cinnamon

Put egg yolks and sugar in top part of a double-boiler and beat with a wire whisk until pale yellow. Gradually add wine. Place mixture over boiling water and beat constantly until it begins to thicken. Do not over-cook; zabaione should be creamy-soft and fluffy. Pour into warmed champagne glasses and serve hot. Serves 6.

CHILLED ZABAIONE WITH LIQUEUR
Zabaione freddo, alla liquore

My favorite liqueur for this dessert is Amaretto di Saronno. Creme de Cacao is another delicious choice.

6 egg yolks
6 tablespoons sugar
½ cup liqueur, see above

Put egg yolks and sugar in top part of a double-boiler; beat with a wire whisk until pale yellow; gradually add liqueur. Place mixture over boiling water and beat constantly until it begins to thicken. Do not over-cook; consistency should be creamy-soft and fluffy. Cool slightly; pour into champagne glasses and chill for 1 hour before serving. Serves 6.

ZABAIONE SOUFFLÉ, TERESA'S WAY
Spuma di zabaione, Teresa

6   egg yolks
⅔   cup sugar
⅔   cup heavy cream
½   cup liqueur such as Galliano, Amaretto di Saronno, Maraschino

Beat together egg yolks and sugar until foamy and light. Cook in double-boiler over boiling water, stirring constantly until mixture is thick but creamy; cool. Whip cream; fold in egg mixture and liqueur. Pour into champagne or sherbet glasses and chill for 1 hour before serving. Very good served with fresh strawberries. Serves 10 to 12.

CHAMPAGNE CUSTARD
Crema allo spumante

6   egg yolks
1   cup dry champagne
½   cup sugar
1   envelope unflavored gelatine
¼   cup cold water
½   cup heavy cream
strawberries or Maraschino cherries

Put egg yolks, champagne, and sugar in top part of double-boiler over simmering water. Cook, stirring until mixture becomes thick and creamy. It will double in bulk. Remove from heat; allow to cool, beating occasionally. Sprinkle gelatine over cold water in a small bowl; place over simmering water until gelatine is dissolved; cool. Fold gelatine into champagne custard. Whip cream until stiff; fold into champagne custard. Pour into six dessert bowls or glasses. Refrigerate for 2 hours before serving. Garnish each serving with a fresh strawberry or a Maraschino cherry. Serves 6.

CHILLED DESSERT "BELVEDERE"
Dolce freddo "Belvedere"

½ cup butter, at room temperature
6 hard-cooked egg yolks (use whites in salad)
½ cup sugar
⅛ teaspoon salt
6 tablespoons rum
36 ladyfingers
1½ cups white Port wine

In container of electric blender, combine butter, egg yolks, sugar, salt, and rum; blend at medium speed for 3 to 4 minutes. Quickly, dip one ladyfinger at a time, into wine; arrange a layer on a serving plate and carefully spread a portion of butter-cream over. Repeat for 3 or 4 layers, ending with a top layer of butter-cream. Cover and refrigerate for 24 hours before serving. Serves 8 to 12.

MASCARPONE (OR CREAM-CHEESE) CUPS
Coppe di Mascarpone

Mascarpone is a creamy and extremely light cheese. It is often served with fruits as dessert. We know that Mascarpone has been popular in the Piemonte region as far back as the 12th century. It is not available in the United States, so here is my Americanized version for you to enjoy.

1 8-ounce package cream cheese, at room temperature
3 egg yolks
¼ cup sugar
4 tablespoons brandy or rum
½ pint heavy cream
strawberries, raspberries, or blueberries for garnish

Beat cheese in blender until smooth and fluffy; add egg yolks, sugar, and brandy or rum; beat for 1 minute longer. Whip cream in a separate bowl; gently fold cheese mixture into whipped cream; spoon into individual dessert cups and garnish with berries. Chill for 2 hours before serving. Serves 6.

RASPBERRIES WITH MARASCHINO CUSTARD
Lamponi con crema al Maraschino

2 whole eggs, well beaten
6 tablespoons sugar
¼ cup Maraschino liqueur
8 ounces fresh or frozen raspberries

Put eggs, 3 tablespoons sugar, and maraschino in top of a double-boiler, over simmering water. Cook, stirring, until mixture becomes thick and creamy. It will double in bulk. Remove from heat and cool. If you are using frozen raspberries, allow them to thaw and drain. Put raspberries through a sieve and discard seeds. Mix remaining 3 tablespoons sugar and raspberry purée until sugar dissolves. Divide purée into four tall sherbet glasses. Top with custard, and refrigerate until serving time. Serves 4.

EGG PASTRY FOR ITALIAN PIES AND TARTS
Pasta frolla per crostata

Crostata is the Italian word for the pastry used for fruit and vegetable pies. The significant difference from the American crust is the use of butter and eggs, instead of fat and water. Whether for dessert or for a main course, Italian pies are always made with a lattice top.

2 cups flour
¾ cup butter, at room temperature
½ cup sugar
½ teaspoon salt
2 whole eggs
2 teaspoons vanilla
2 teaspoons grated fresh lemon rind

In a bowl, combine flour, butter, sugar, salt, eggs, vanilla, and lemon rind. Work mixture with your hands until mixed; shape into a smooth ball; cover tightly and refrigerate for 30 minutes to 1 hour. When crust is made to be used with vegetables, omit sugar, vanilla, and lemon rind; proceed in the same manner. Makes dough for one 10-inch bottom crust and one lattice top.

THREE FRUITS PIE
Crostata tre frutti

Preheat oven to 400°F.
1 recipe for Egg Pastry, page 186
4 large Bartlett pears, unpeeled, cored and sliced
½ cup dried currants
1 cup dried apricots, chopped
3 tablespoons butter
½ cup apricot jam
1 egg yolk
1 tablespoon water
1 tablespoon sugar

Filling: In a bowl combine pears, currants, apricots, and butter; mix well. Remove dough from refrigerator; divide into two pieces; roll one piece with rolling pin on a lightly floured surface to ⅛ inch thick, and about 12 inches round; very gently transfer to a buttered and floured 10-inch fluted pie pan. Prick bottom with a fork and bake for 10 minutes. Remove from oven; spoon apricot jam over and spoon pear mixture on top of jam. Roll out second piece of dough slightly thicker for the lattice top. Cut into ¾-inch strips. Lay half of the strips 1 inch apart over filling. Weave remaining strips in the opposite direction, in a diamond or square pattern. Beat egg with water; brush gently over strips. Sprinkle with sugar and bake for 20 minutes, then, cover top with aluminum foil, to prevent pastry from becoming too brown; pastry should have a nice golden color. Bake 10 minutes more. Let stand 2 to 3 hours before serving at room temperature. Serves 6 to 8.

PURÉED FRUIT FILLING FOR PIES AND SMALL TARTS
Marmellata per crostate

5	Bartlett pears
5	apples
1	whole lemon
1	whole orange
1	cup dried apricots, diced
2	teaspoons almond extract

Wash fresh fruit; do not peel but core and slice pears and apples; quarter lemon and orange. In a large saucepan, combine pears, apples, lemon, orange, apricots, and almond extract; cover and simmer over low heat for 2 hours. Remove from heat and cool. Pour into electric blender and purée for a few seconds. Filling stores well in the refrigerator up to two weeks. Makes filling for 2 pies.

MARMALADE PIE
Crostata di marmellata

Preheat oven to 400°F.

1	recipe for Egg Pastry, page 186
1	pound Seville orange or your favorite flavor marmalade
1	egg yolk
1	tablespoon cold water
1	tablespoon sugar

Remove dough from refrigerator; divide it into two pieces; with rolling pin, roll one piece on a lightly floured surface, ⅛ inch thick to fit a 10-inch fluted pie pan. Prick bottom with a fork; bake for 10 minutes. Remove from oven; spoon marmalade into shell and spread evenly. Roll out second piece of dough slightly thicker for lattice top. Cut into 8 to 10 strips ¾ inch wide. Lay half of the strips over filling one inch apart. Weave remaining strips in opposite direction, in diamond or square pattern. Beat egg yolk with water; brush gently over strips. Sprinkle with sugar and bake for 15 or 20 minutes, until strips are golden. Let stand 2 to 3 hours before serving at room temperature. Serves 6 to 8.

FRESH GRAPE PIE
Crostata d'uva

Preheat oven to 400°F.

1½ cups white seedless grapes, stemmed
1½ cups dark grapes, seeded and stemmed
4   tablespoons Kirsch liqueur
½   recipe for Egg Pastry, page 186
1   cup apricot jam

Wash and drain grapes; place in a bowl; prick each grape with a fork; pour Kirsch over and toss; set aside to marinate for 1 hour. Remove dough from refrigerator; with rolling pin, on a lightly floured surface, roll dough ⅛ inch thick, into a circle to fit a 10-inch fluted pie pan. Very gently transfer it to buttered and floured pan. Prick bottom with a fork and bake for 20 minutes. Remove from oven and cool completely. Spread ½ cup apricot jam over bottom of crust; drain grapes; press grapes into jam to make a two-colored checkerboard design. Over low heat, melt remaining ½ cup apricot jam; brush on grapes to form a glaze. Chill for 1 hour before serving. Serves 6 to 8.

PEACH PIE
Crostata di pesche

Preheat oven to 400°F.

½   recipe for Egg Pastry, page 186
1   cup currant jelly
3   cups sliced, fresh or canned peaches
3   tablespoons cinnamon sugar
2   tablespoons butter

Remove dough from refrigerator; roll with rolling pin on a lightly floured surface to ⅛ inch thick in a circle to fit pan. Very gently transfer to a buttered and floured 10-inch fluted pie pan. Prick bottom with a fork and bake for 10 minutes. Remove from oven; spoon and spread jelly over. Arrange peaches over jelly in a spiral design; sprinkle with sugar; dot with butter. Bake for 20 minutes. Serve hot or cold. Serves 6 to 8.

PEAR PIE
Crostata di pere

Preheat oven to 400°F.

- 6 large Bartlett pears, unpeeled, cored and sliced
- 6 tablespoons sugar
- 4 tablespoons butter, melted
- 2 tablespoons fresh lemon juice
- 1 recipe for Egg Pastry, page 186
- 1 egg yolk
- 1 tablespoon water
- 1 tablespoon sugar

Filling: In a bowl combine pears, 6 tablespoons sugar, butter, and lemon juice; mix well. Remove dough from refrigerator; divide into two pieces; roll one piece with rolling pin on a lightly-floured surface to ⅛ inch thick to fit pie pan; very gently transfer to a buttered and floured 10-inch fluted pie pan. Prick bottom with a fork and bake for 10 minutes. Remove from oven; spoon pear mixture into shell and spread evenly. Roll out second piece of dough, slightly thicker for the lattice top. Cut into 8 or 10 strips, ¾ inches wide. Lay half of the strips over pears, one inch apart. Weave remaining strips in the opposite direction, in diamond or square pattern. Beat egg yolk with water; brush gently over strips. Sprinkle with sugar. Bake for 20 minutes; then, cover top with a piece of aluminum foil to prevent pastry from becoming too brown. Bake 10 minutes longer. Pastry should have a nice golden color. Let stand 2 or 3 hours before serving at room temperature. Serves 6 or 8.

BAKED PEARS
Pere al forno alla Piemontese

Preheat oven to 350°F.

- 2 pounds Anjou or Bartlett pears
- 2 cups robust red wine (If you feel like splurging, use Barolo)
- ½ cup sugar
- ⅛ teaspoon cinnamon
- 6 cloves
- 4 1-inch pieces lemon rind, yellow part only

Wash pears; arrange in a bake-and-serve dish; pour wine over; sprinkle with sugar and cinnamon; add cloves and lemon rind to wine in dish. Bake for 30 to 40 minutes, until pears are tender. Serves 6.

BAKED STUFFED PEACHES ALLA PIEMONTESE

Pesche ripiene, alla Piemontese

Preheat oven to 350°F.

- 6 large ripe peaches
- 6 medium-size amaretti (Italian macaroons) crumbled
- 2 egg yolks
- 3 tablespoons sugar
- 2 tablespoons Kirsch or Maraschino liqueur
- 2 tablespoons cocoa (optional)
- 3 tablespoons butter

Wash peaches; cut in half; remove stones and scoop out most of the pulp, leaving a shell. Chop peach pulp; in a bowl, combine pulp with macaroons, egg yolks, sugar, liqueur, cocoa, and mix well. Fill peach shells with the mixture. Arrange peaches in a buttered bake-and-serve dish; dot with butter and bake for 30 minutes. Serve hot or cold. Serves 6.

APPLES OR PEARS IN A "SHIRT"

Mele o pere in camicia

When I was a very young girl in the "Belvedere's" kitchen, often I was given a piece of egg pastry to do with what I liked. Frequently I would wrap it around an apple or pear, rub it with butter; sprinkle it with sugar and bake it. Eventually I worked out a more sophisticated recipe than that simple, yet memorable dessert.

Preheat oven to 375°F.

- ½ cup apricot jam
- ½ cup ground blanched almonds
- 2 tablespoons butter
- 6 apples or pears, peeled (if possible leave the stems)
- 2 tablespoons sugar
- 1 recipe for Egg Pastry, page 186
- 1 egg, beaten

In a small bowl, combine jam, almonds, and butter, mix well. Core apples or pears, from the bottom, leaving the stems. Fill with jam-almond mixture. Remove pastry from refrigerator and roll out ⅛ inch thick. Cut out six 7-inch circles. Wrap each fruit with a pastry circle. Brush with beaten egg; sprinkle with sugar. Bake for 25 to 30 minutes, or until pastry turns golden. Serve warm or cold. Serves 6.

BAKED STUFFED PEARS
Pere ripiene al forno

Preheat oven to 350°F.

- 6 large Anjou pears
- ⅓ cup brown sugar
- 6 large amaretti (Italian macaroons) crumbled
- 2 teaspoons grated fresh orange rind
- 1 teaspoon orange flower water
- 2 egg yolks
- ¼ cup dry white wine

Do not peel pears; wash and cut in half lengthwise; core and scoop out a hole the size of a walnut; sprinkle with brown sugar. In a small bowl combine amaretti, orange rind, orange water, and egg yolks; mix well. Fill pear halves with mixture; arrange in a baking dish; pour wine into dish and bake for 25 to 45 minutes, until pears are soft to the touch. Serve hot or cold. Serves 6.

FRIED AMARETTI (ITALIAN MACAROONS)
Amaretti fritti

- 12 medium-size amaretti, Italian macaroons
- 1 egg, well beaten
- ½ cup unflavored breadcrumbs
- 4 tablespoons butter
- 2 tablespoons oil

Dip amaretti into egg, then into breadcrumbs. Melt butter in a large skillet; add oil and fry amaretti for 1 minute on each side. Serve hot. Serves 6.

APPLE FRITTERS
Frittelle di mele

  6 large sweet apples
  4 tablespoons Kirsch
  1 tablespoon fresh lemon juice
1½ cups flour
  3 tablespoons baking powder
¼ teaspoon salt
  4 tablespoons sugar
  1 cup milk
  2 eggs, beaten
oil for frying
confectioner's sugar (optional)

Peel and core apples; cut into small pieces; pour liqueur and lemon juice over; mix and let marinate at room temperature for 30 minutes. Add flour, baking powder, salt, sugar, milk, and eggs; stir to mix. Pour ½ inch of oil into a frying pan and turn the heat to medium-high. Drop apple-batter mixture by tablespoonsful into hot oil; when fritters turn golden on one side, turn them. When both sides are golden brown, remove from oil and transfer to paper towels to drain. If desired, sprinkle with confectioner's sugar before serving. Serve hot. Serves 6.

LIES— PIEMONTESE FRIED PASTRY
Bugie

This pastry is known by many names, *cenci, nodi, chiacchere, lattughe, galani,* and *sfrappole.* In Piemonte they are called *bugie,* or lies, because, they say, as with lies, you cannot stop after the first one.

  3 cups flour
  5 tablespoons butter, melted
¼ cup sugar
  3 teaspoons baking powder
  4 egg yolks
  3 tablespoons rum
½ cup milk
¼ teaspoon cinnamon
oil for frying
confectioner's sugar

In a bowl, combine flour, butter, sugar, baking powder, egg yolks, rum, milk, and cinnamon; with your hands, work into a hard dough; wrap and refrigerate for 1 hour. Place dough on a floured surface; cut into 2 or 3 pieces. Roll each piece, one at a time, into a sheet about ⅛ inch thick; cut with pastry wheel into 2 4-inch strips. Twist each strip into a knot; fry, a few at a time, in hot oil. When they are puffed and golden, remove from oil, and drain on paper towels. Transfer to a serving platter and sprinkle with confectioner's sugar. Serve warm. Serves 12.

SWEET FRIED SEMOLINA
Frittura dolce

1 quart milk
1 cup cream of wheat, often called farina
3 egg yolks
½ teaspoon salt
¼ teaspoon sugar
grated rind of one lemon
2 tablespoons almond extract
2 whole eggs
½ cup flour
1 cup unflavored breadcrumbs
6 tablespoons butter
6 tablespoons oil

In a saucepan, heat milk just to boiling; lower heat, add cream of wheat, a little at a time, constantly stirring with a wooden spoon until cream of wheat is all in saucepan; continue cooking and stirring for 10 minutes longer. Remove from heat; rapidly mix in egg yolks, salt, sugar, lemon rind, and almond extract. Oil a flat surface and spread mixture 1-inch thick; cool. The mixture should be made, up to this point, and refrigerated, the day before you wish to use it; mixture is easier to cut when chilled. Cut crosswise into diamond-shaped pieces, about 2 inches long. Beat 2 whole eggs; dredge pieces in flour; shake off excess; dip into eggs and dredge in breadcrumbs; shake off excess. In a large skillet melt butter over medium heat; add oil. Fry pieces until golden brown. Remove and place on paper towels to drain. Serve hot. Serves 6 to 8.

HAZELNUT NUGGETS, MINIATURE MACAROONS
Nocciolini di Chivasso

Chivasso is a town outside of Torino.

Preheat oven to 350°F.
- 8 ounces hazelnuts
- 6 tablespoons confectioner's sugar
- 3 egg whites, well beaten
- dash of salt
- 1 teaspoon vanilla extract

Roll hazelnuts between the palms of your hands, to rub off the thin skins. Grind hazelnuts. Add sugar, and stir. Fold in egg whites, salt, and vanilla. With a pastry bag, using ½-inch nozzle, drop dough in small mounds onto a well-greased and floured baking sheet. Bake for 8 to 10 minutes or until golden brown. Remove very carefully with a spatula, and cool. Makes about 4 to 5 dozen.

LADYFINGERS
Savoiardi, Piemontesi Ladyfingers

Preheat oven to 350°F.
- 1 cup flour
- 1¼ cups confectioner's sugar
- ¼ teaspoon salt
- 6 eggs, separated
- 1 teaspoon almond extract

Sift together flour, half of the sugar, and salt; set aside. Beat egg yolks with remaining sugar until creamy and light in color; add almond extract. Beat egg whites until stiff; fold into egg yolk mixture. Fold in flour mixture, a little at a time. With pastry bag, using 1-inch nozzle, shape into 4-inch strips on a well-greased and floured baking sheet. Bake for 10 to 12 minutes, or until lightly golden. Remove very carefully with a spatula and cool on wire rack. Makes about 3 dozen.

COFFEE
Caffè

Espresso is the favorite coffee of all Italians. For home use, it is made with a special, steam-pressure machine, available in gourmet shops. For best results you should make coffee according to the directions given with the machine.

After dinner, often one teaspoon of rum or cognac is added to each cup of espresso coffee, for a more buoyant flavor.

Very often in the morning you will be served *Capuccino* coffee and milk. It is easy to make and very good. To make Capuccino, use 2 pots, one with hot espresso coffee, the other with hot milk. Pour them simultaneously into the cup, to blend. Add sugar to taste.

General Index

Agnolotti, Signor Antonio, sauce
 for, 66
Amaretti, fried (Italian macaroons),
 192
Anchovy:
 baked peppers with, 4
 fillets in green sauce, 7–8
 hot, garlic dip, 6
 scaloppine with, 91–92
Antipasto, royal, "Belvedere,"
 17–18
Appetizers:
 anchovy canapés, 9
 anchovy fillets in green sauce, 7–8
 baked peppers with anchovies, 4
 canapés, 8
 celery salad Signor Antonio, 12
 cheese canapés, 9
 cheese puffs, two, 14–15
 chicken liver canapés "Belvedere,"
 8
 chicken salad "Belvedere," 7
 cold rice mold, 15
 crespelle with truffles, 16–17
 garlic bread Piemontese, 5
 ham rolls in aspic, 10–11
 hot anchovy and garlic dip, 6

Italian prosciutto, irresistible, 3–4
 mushroom canapés, 9
 mushroom salad Papá
 Constantino, 13–14
 pickled green onions (scallions),
 4–5
 pickled mushrooms, 15–16
 plums with bacon alla Laura, 5
 prosciutto and asparagus rolls, 3
 raw beef:
  and mushroom salad Signor
  Antonio, 19–20
  salad Laura, 19
  salad Piemontese, 18–19
 roasted pepper with Bagna Caôda,
 6
 royal antipasto "Belvedere," 17–18
 Russian salad, 10
 stuffed artichoke hearts, 12–13
 stuffed mushrooms alla
 Valdostana, 13
 tomatoes stuffed with Russian
 salad, 11
 tuna fish foam, 16
 vegetable appetizer platter, 11–12
 whimsical salad, 7
Apple fritters, 193

Apples or pears, in a "shirt," 191–
 192
Artichoke:
 hearts, stuffed, 12–13
 stuffed, alla Torinese, 156
Asparagus:
 cold, with tuna fish, 157
 prosciutto and, rolls, 3
 sautéed, 158
 scrumptious, 156–157
 with butter and cheese, 158
Aspic:
 brandied, chicken roll in, 134–135
 chicken, 135–136
 fish in, 76–77
 ham rolls in, 10–11
Asti's bean soup, 31
Avocado sauce, beef fillets with, 99

Bacon, plums with, alla Laura, 5
Bagna Caôda:
 potato dumplings with, 57
 roasted pepper with, 6
Barley and beef soup, 27–28
Barolo, braised beef with, 84
Bean soup, Asti's, 31

Italian Index

About the Author

Teresa Gilardi Candler, a native of Torino, Italy, has been a citizen of the United States since 1961. Teresa is the food editor for the *North Jersey Suburbanite,* and food columnist for several weekly and monthly papers. In her spare time she is a bridal consultant. She is married, has a son, Peter, a college student, and lives in Closter, New Jersey, with her husband Gerry.

The author's major interests include people, fashion, and food. Teresa's mother taught her the art of Northern Italian cooking. Chefs in her father's restaurant added highlights to her *arte culinaria* education. Fans of her cooking include notables such as Craig Claiborne. Teresa is also the author of *Good 'n' Easy Cooking for Singles.* She is now at work on a volume, *How to Cook Vegetables the Italian Way.*